BRITISH BIRDS

by Robert Dougall

Photographs by
Natural History Photographic Agency and Aquila

Illustrations by Hilary Jarvis

Ladybird Books Loughborough

Introduction

It's strange to think now that for about half my life I must have been walking about with my eyes shut. How else to explain that I was over thirty years old before I became fully aware of the immense variety, wonder and beauty of birdlife all around me.

My early boyhood was spent in the Surrey suburbs in the 1920s. The attitude to birds in Britain then was very different from what it is today. Most of my friends made collections of birds' eggs, which were then shut away in drawers or cigar boxes and looked to me rather dreary. Today, it is against the law to take the eggs of any bird, except those of a very few which are classed as pests. That is progress.

We now know that it is much more interesting to watch birds flying about – to marvel at the beauty and variety of their plumage, to observe their ways on land or water, study their migration, admire the devotion to their young and perhaps, above all, take delight in bird song.

In my case, it was not until after the last war that my eyes were opened to the wonders of birdlife. Walking along the deserted Suffolk beaches, my attention was caught by those elegant seabirds the Little Terns as, in buoyant flight, with bills downturned, they endlessly

Avocet

scanned the waves. Every now and again one of these 'sea swallows' would hover daintily for a few seconds before plummeting down with a splash. It was seldom that one would re-appear without a tiny fish glinting silver in its bill. These are exceptionally fascinating birds to watch, but I must have seen them in different places hundreds of times before without paying them any particular attention. This time there was no other distraction so I watched with delight and soon found myself well and truly hooked on a new leisure interest.

I suppose that after the destruction and ugliness of the war years, I was in a receptive mood. In any case, it was an exciting time to be in Suffolk, because a few kilometres down the coast that most elegant of all wading birds, the black and white Avocet with long upswept bill, had returned after a hundred years to nest in Britain.

I promptly joined the Royal Society for the Protection of Birds, which then had only about six thousand members. Little did I think that twenty years later I should be invited to become the President of the Society, which, by then, had a membership of more than two hundred thousand. Today, it's more like three hundred and fifty thousand with another hundred and ten thousand in the junior branch – the Young Ornithologists' Club. That's nearly half a million people of all ages in Britain taking an active interest in the protection of birdlife – and the RSPB is only one of many conservation bodies. This, it seems to me, is one aspect of life in which our country can take great pride.

One of the attractions of birdwatching as an interest is that you can follow it almost anywhere – in country or town, on holiday or on special expeditions – and, most important of all, in your own garden or local park. And it costs very little money. All you need in the way of equipment is a good pair of eyes, binoculars, a bird book for identification, a notebook in which to jot down points about the birds you see and some good stout walking shoes or gum boots. The binoculars are fairly expensive, but they will last a lifetime with care and there is a wide range of prices. It is probably better to avoid second-hand ones, unless you get expert advice.

Then it is a good idea to join the Young Ornithologists' Club of the RSPB or your County Naturalists' Trust or the Wildfowl Trust. The YOC make a point of arranging interesting projects on the study of birds and their protection. To give you an idea, they not so long ago organised a search of the banks of rivers, lakes and canals to collect the nylon thread thrown away or left

4

behind by anglers. If any unsuspecting bird should get entangled in this, it very often dies a slow death by strangulation or loses a limb. As a result of the YOC's search, several kilometres of fishing line were recovered and many birds spared a lingering death or disablement.

The County Naturalists' Trusts also arrange for their members to take part in practical conservation work on their own nature reserves, such as clearing scrub, reopening overgrown ponds and clearing streams of rubbish. The Trusts are now controlled by an overall body called the Royal Society for Nature Conservation.

Many people first take an interest in birds by watching them at their garden bird-tables. Then, they may start wondering about them. For instance, what were their origins? At a glance, there's little to connect everybody's favourite the friendly little Robin with a reptile, but there's no doubt that the whole great family of birds we know today can be traced back to a strange-looking creature roughly the size of a Magpie. It lived about a hundred and forty million years ago and combined the characteristics of bird and reptile: it was the first creature to have feathers. The chances are that it was unable to fly properly,

An artist's reconstruction of what the bird may have looked like

owing to the weak structure of the breastbone. There were three claws on the curve of each wing and with the help of these it was probably able to drag itself up to the topmost branches and launch itself in a glide to the next tree. Another indicator is that its bones were not hollow like those of the birds we know today. This extra weight would probably restrict it to gliding.

How do we know all this? Well, it was thanks to a chance discovery in a limestone quarry in Bavaria in 1861. A man working there split a

stone in two and noticed a weird shape with the clear imprint of feathers. Fortunately, experts were called in, who realised that they were looking at the fossil remains of the first bird-like creature from ancient times. Later that year, a skeleton was found. The remains were acquired by the Natural History Department of the British Museum and given the scientific name

ARCHAEOPTERYX LITHOGRAPHICA.

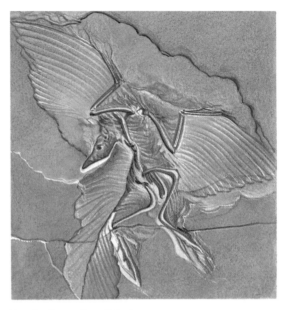

The fossil remains of Archaeopteryx

There was immense interest and excitement because birds scarcely ever become fossilised: the body structure is so light and fragile that it rapidly disintegrates. The only exception is when a bird's body falls into deposits on the bed of a slow-running river or tranquil lake. The fossil of Archaeopteryx was found in slate, formed from silt at the bottom of a lake. It was evidence that the birds we know today have gradually evolved over hundreds of millions of years.

In the British Isles, with its variable climate and vegetation and long irregular coastline, there are many varied types of locality or habitat in which over two hundred kinds of bird can breed. For the purposes of this book I have grouped them into six main habitats:

Gardens and Woods;

Heaths and Farmland;

Rivers, Lakes, Gravel pits and Reservoirs;

Forests, Mountains and Moors;

Estuaries and Marshes;

Coasts and Cliffs.

Before we look at the individual birds, let's think of some clues that will help us to distinguish the different species. It's rather like being a detective.

All the different groups of birds have evolved and adapted to suit their particular ways of living and getting food. Some birds eat vegetable matter like seeds, fruit, buds and leaves; others take animal food such as small mammals, fish, snails, insects and worms.

Each family of birds has developed the type of beak best suited to deal with the kind of food it eats. Some that eat a wide variety of food have a 'general purpose' beak. The Song Thrush is a

Song Thrush

good example: it likes to eat worms, slugs, snails, insects and berries so it has a medium-sized, sharp beak, which can deal with all items of its diet. You may have seen a thrush holding a snail in its bill and smashing the shell against a stone, which it uses as a tiny anvil.

Then there are the seed-eating birds, the finches, which have short thick bills for breaking the outer casing of seeds. The Hawfinch has a particularly strong bill because it likes to eat the

Hawfinch

soft kernel inside a cherry stone. It takes a pressure of about forty kilograms to crack the stone, so its bill really does pack a punch.

Other birds, like the Swift and the Nightjar, live by scooping up flying insects on the wing and so they have huge gaping bills. The Nightjar even has a mouth fringed with bristles so that, once caught, the moth or other insect has little chance of escape.

The woodpecker family need specialised pick-axe-like bills to dig holes in trees and to chisel into bark for insects. They also have long tongues which can shoot out to nearly four times the length of the beaks. With these they can lick into the holes and the ends of their tongues have backward-pointing barbs with which to draw out the insects.

Other birds, like the Heron, have long dagger-like bills for plunging into water or mud and grabbing fish. The bills of most fish-eating birds, especially the saw-bill ducks, have serrations like backward-pointing teeth for grasping and holding their slippery prey. Surface-feeding ducks like the Shoveler have wide flat bills for scooping up water or mud and filtering the food from it.

The powerful, hooked beak of the bird of prey for tearing at flesh is one of the best examples of a specialised bill, but I expect you can think of many others.

Birds' legs and feet are also specially adapted to suit the life they lead. Obviously, birds which feed by wading in water need long legs: the Heron is a good example. At the other extreme, Swifts, which live almost entirely in the air, scarcely use their legs at all. In fact they only land on the ground by accident and then they are so helpless that they can be easily caught. On the other hand, they can cling to almost vertical surfaces by using their four forward-facing toes as hooks.

Swimming birds have their legs set well back on the body for the same reason that a ship has the propeller at the stern — in that position it provides the maximum thrust through the water. The result is that on land some of them can scarcely walk at all. Their feet are either webbed like the ducks or else they have paddle-shaped toes or lobes, as in the Grebe family.

I expect you have noticed from watching the birds in your garden or park that some birds hop and others walk or run. The Blackbird, which spends much of its time moving about in trees and bushes, is one of the hopping variety, while Starlings, which spend more time on the ground, find walking more efficient.

Unlike us, birds have only four toes; usually one points backwards, the other three forwards. With perching birds the hind toe helps to clamp it to a branch. Have you ever wondered why birds don't fall off a branch when they go to sleep? It is simply that when the bird settles, tendons down the back of the legs pull taut and the toes curl in tight. They stay that way until the bird raises itself upright again and the tension on the tendons is automatically released. As with the legs, there are many variations in birds' toes too. Woodpeckers have two toes pointing backwards and two forwards. This makes it easier for them to climb trees by gripping the bark. The Partridge scarcely has a hind toe at all — it is only a stub. This is because it runs a lot and, like a sprinter, all the weight is thrown forward and taken by the front three toes.

Then there are the birds of prey, which use their powerful hooked claws not only for perching, but also for seizing and sometimes killing their prey. That magnificent fish-hawk, the Osprey, has small spines on the pads of its feet so that after its plunge into the water with those deadly talons it can continue to hold the writhing fish.

Most important of all for birds are their wings. It is essential that they should have the wings best suited to their particular way of life. For speed, long thin, swept-back wings are best. The Swift is a good example. It can fly at ninety-six kilometres an hour, climb to eighteen hundred metres and is even thought to sleep on the wing. The Peregrine falcon is probably the fastest of all our birds with a speed of over 160 kph in a dive on its victim.

In contrast, large birds of prey like the Buzzard need long, broad wings for soaring. The deeply slotted wing-tips and wide, rounded tail enable it to hover and manoeuvre with mastery in the air, as it pin-points its victim below, before making the final pounce.

Have you ever walked along a cliff-top and seen how Black-backed Gulls or Fulmars glide along beside you, as though they were suspended in air? They are making use of the updraughts. Long, narrow wings are best for gliding and the Fulmars in particular are expert.

There seems no limit to the adaptability of birds. Who would have dreamt fifty years ago that a falcon like the Kestrel would become quite a common sight in our towns and cities. It was only in the 1930s that it first started nesting in central London. The bird has also learnt that motorway verges and embankments make ideal hunting grounds. The lack of disturbance and absence of agricultural chemical sprays mean that

Kestrel

small mammals and insects abound there. Other birds of prey need high perching places but not the Kestrel, which has the ability to hover. How fascinating it is to watch the skill with which it heads into the wind and holds its position over a certain spot by flying at exactly the same speed as the wind.

Every day, wherever we are in Britain, the marvels of birdlife are all around us. In this country, unlike some parts of Europe, wild birds are not particularly afraid of man but they are wary, of course, and may not allow a close inspection. When birdwatching, always remember to move about slowly, even when raising binoculars to your eyes. If you stand or sit completely still birds will often come quite close. When a bird suddenly darts across a clearing without giving you a chance of a good look, don't get annoyed, but just stay completely still. Remember that birds are very often in pairs or small flocks and there's every likelihood that another of the same species will follow.

So — happy birdwatching! And make sure you don't spend half your life with your eyes shut — as I did.

Robert Dougall

Migration

For thousands of years mankind has marvelled at the mass movements of some of the birds each autumn and spring. It was noticed in particular that Swallows, with the approach of autumn, gathered in flocks usually near water or reedbeds. They moved in the direction of the coast and then suddenly one day they were gone. But where? Right up to the 18th century, some serious naturalists still thought that the birds passed the winter rolled up together to form a ball, in the mud, at the bottom of ponds. That wasn't the only strange idea: Storks and some other birds were even thought to spend the winter on the moon.

It is easy for us to laugh now but, after all, there was no proof of where they went. This did not come until bird-ringing was started at the end of the last century. A light metal ring was fastened to the bird's leg; it had on it a number and an address. In the course of time, recoveries of dead birds, which had been ringed in this way, were made all over the world and in many cases the rings were returned. This provided the evidence to show where the birds went.

Bird-ringing is still carried on today and continues to provide much information. It is organised by the British Trust for Ornithology. Each British ring, besides a number, carries the address: Brit. Museum, London S.W.7. Foreign ringing stations have their own addresses. The French, for instance, put this address on their bird-rings: OIS. MUSEUM, PARIS. So, if ever you find a dead bird with a ring on its leg, make sure that you return the ring, with all the information you can give, to the right address. In this way, you will be helping to add to the knowledge about the movements of birds.

It has been estimated that a hundred and twenty million land birds fly into Britain each year to raise their families. Most of them spend the winter in the Mediterranean countries or further south. Six million Swallows make the journey to and from South Africa. It takes them six weeks to make the ten thousand kilometre journey.

Of all our seabirds the greatest distance is covered by the Arctic Terns. They nest not only in the north of Britain, but right up to the Arctic Circle, within a few hundred kilometres of the North Pole. Twice a year, they cover the astonishing distance of sixteen thousand kilometres between the North and South Poles. In this way, Arctic Terns get more hours of daylight than any other creature in the world.

The Arctic Tern, champion long-distance flyer

The main motive for birds' movements is to be sure of a good supply of food. As winter approaches in Britain, there are fewer insects on which birds feed, also fewer seeds and berries and shorter hours of daylight in which to find them. So − off they go to the sun.

The tiny Sedge Warbler, for instance, flies to its wintering quarters in Africa, south of the Sahara Desert, a distance of four thousand kilometres in four days and nights of non-stop flying. In order to be able to do this, it has to double its body fat in the weeks beforehand, much as an aircraft has to take on fuel. How does the little creature know when to start preparing? Evidently, birds must have some kind of internal clock to trigger them off, but this process is not yet fully understood. This internal clock probably also helps the bird to find its way.

As I expect you know, if you point the hour hand of your watch at the sun, a line bisecting the angle between the hour hand and 12 o'clock will point due south. Other directions follow from that. So, birds navigate by the sun in the daytime, or by the stars at night, and probably with the help of some kind of internal clock. It is also possible that they make use in some way of the earth's magnetic field. There is fascination in the thought that although we are now able to land men on the moon, there is much we still have to learn about the mysteries of bird migration.

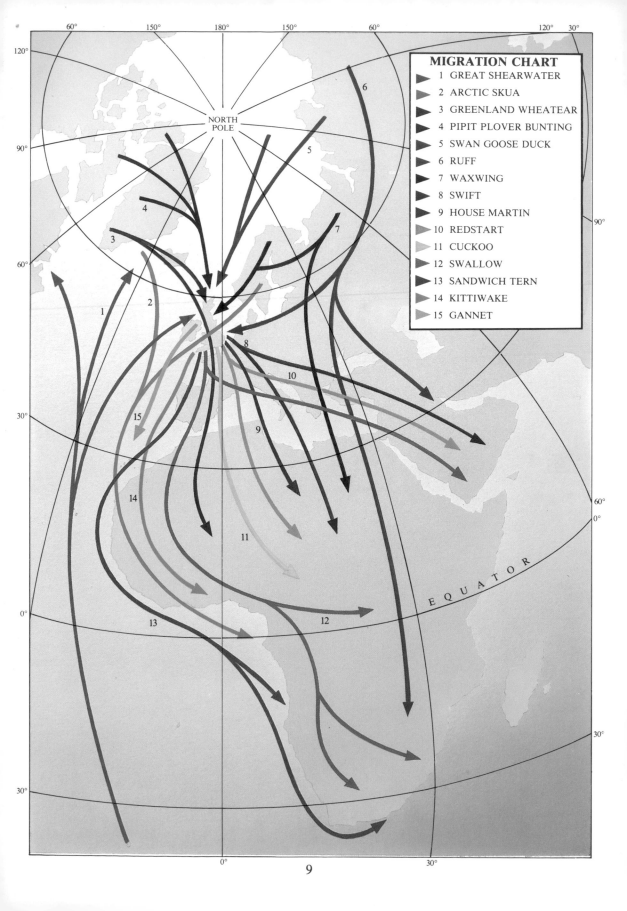

MIGRATION CHART

1 GREAT SHEARWATER
2 ARCTIC SKUA
3 GREENLAND WHEATEAR
4 PIPIT PLOVER BUNTING
5 SWAN GOOSE DUCK
6 RUFF
7 WAXWING
8 SWIFT
9 HOUSE MARTIN
10 REDSTART
11 CUCKOO
12 SWALLOW
13 SANDWICH TERN
14 KITTIWAKE
15 GANNET

NORTH POLE

EQUATOR

9

Recognition in flight

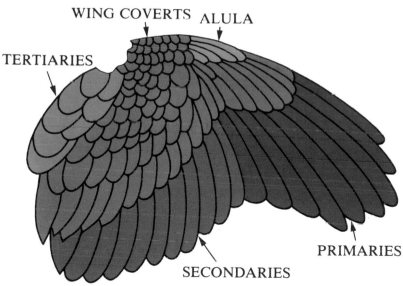

TERTIARIES

WING COVERTS   ALULA

PRIMARIES

SECONDARIES

Wing
Showing the different feathers, primaries, secondaries, tertiaries, coverts and alula. The latter is made up of three or four short feathers attached to the 'thumb'. These normally lie flat but are extended when flying at low speed to prevent stalling.
(see Landing techniques)

◀ *MANX SHEARWATER*
Small body, long pointed wings, black upper, white lower, wings held stiffly, gliding and banking in flight using available air currents. Clumsy on land and has to scramble up rocks to gain height for take-off.

FULMAR ▶
Heavy body, short neck, grey above, white underneath, distinctive underwing pattern. Similar gliding and banking flight to Shearwater. Feet usually tucked into feathers to assist streamlining.

◀ *GANNET*
Adult white, with long, dark-tipped wings which have a wing span of two metres. Young dark, later brown and white. Long neck and tail, narrow body. When diving, often drop vertically thirty metres or more, normally folding wings right back before entry into water.

SHAG ▶
Black plumage with satin green tinge; long neck; crest in spring and summer with yellow gape patch. Mainly low flying. Rarely goes inland. Sexes alike. Both Shag and Cormorant (below) land with an ungraceful flop.

◀ *CORMORANT*
Black with green gloss; white patch on face and flanks in breeding season. Large and awkward in flight, can soar to great heights, often doing so inland. Sexes alike.

LAPWING ▶
Only indigenous medium-sized black and white bird with rounded wings and short tail. In bright sunlight can look brilliant green on upper parts. Long thin crest, slow wing-beat. Sexes alike but female has narrower body.

10

AVOCET

Largely white with black cap and wing-tips, long legs trail in flight. Wings rounder in flight than most waders. Long upturned bill and narrow black chevrons on upper body make identification easy. Sexes alike.

OYSTERCATCHER ▶

In flight, white underside and black and white wing and tail markings make for easy identification. Long orange bill, pink legs. Young have grey-tipped bill and white collar. Adults develop collar in winter. Sexes alike.

◀ BITTERN

Buff plumage streaked and barred black and brown. Broad wings. Long green legs trail in flight. Rare outside East Anglia, a few nest in Kent, Lancashire and Wales. Sexes alike.

GREY HERON ▶

Slow ponderous flight, legs trailing; long drawn-in neck produces conspicuous bulge. Grey upper parts, dark grey flight feathers, black crest, bushy breastplate, strong yellow bill. Sexes alike.

◀ KESTREL

Small and slim with pointed wings, long tail. In adult male, tail is plain grey with broad black band. Only predator which hovers (far left). Now seen along motorway margins at heights between 10–30 metres. Tail angle constantly adjusted to windspeed. Characteristic manner of rising before hover (left).

◀ PEREGRINE

Body bulkier than other falcons. Long tail, long pointed wings. Male – slate coloured back, barred underparts, heavy black moustaches. Female – larger and browner. Distinctive flight alternates rapid flapping with long glides. Left – stooping to attack from above.

◀ BUZZARD

Broad wings and wide rounded medium length tail. Common Buzzard soars with wings held farther forward than Honey Buzzard. Plumage variable, identifiable by broad round wings and patch marking.

RED KITE
Slender body, rusty brown plumage with streaked white head, female slightly duller. Slender wings bent sharply backwards in flight. Pale wing patch prominent. Deeply forked tail (far left) almost vanishes in soaring (left).

SPARROWHAWK
Broad wings with rounded ends, small head and square tail. Adult male has brownish-red barred underparts and is smaller than female, which has browner upperparts, dark brown bars on lower parts, white stripe behind eye. Fast direct flight. Sometimes soars.

◀ GREENFINCH (male)
Plump body, olive green plumage, long wings with yellow wing-bar and tail sides. Heavy pale bill. Erratic bounding flight typical of other finches. Young and females have darker colouring but always show same yellow patches on wings and tail.

GOLDFINCH ▲
Very small. In flight vivid and unique yellow pattern on wings is distinctive. Brown-black plumage, black and white tail. Red face, rest of head black and white. Sexes alike.

◀ SISKIN (male)
Very small, long wings, short tail – all noticeable in flight. Yellow-green plumage, bright yellow wing-bars, dark streaks on back and flanks. Male has black bib and crown. Female more drab and no yellow patch on tail.

◀ BRAMBLING
White rump, orange-buff breast and shoulder patch in male. Male's head and upper parts glossy black in summer, mottled brown in winter. Female has dull brown upper parts. Very similar to Chaffinch.

LINNET (male) ▲
Chestnut back, white wing-bar, white sides to forked tail. Male has crimson crown and breast in summer. Female duller with more streaking. White markings on wings and tail identify both sexes and all ages.

TAWNY OWL
Short rounded wings, large head, short tail, round facial disc, very large dark eyes. Swift, agile, undulating flight. Wing-beats interspersed with glides. Best seen at dawn. Sexes alike.

BARN OWL
Golden-buff plumage, white face and underparts, female slightly more grey. Large head, short square tail and medium-long wings. Slow, slightly wavering flight. Can be seen in daylight, especially when feeding young.

LITTLE OWL
Grey-brown plumage, barred and mottled with white, rounded wings, short tail, round short body, underside heavily barred. Bright yellow eyes, black centres. Bouncing undulating flight. Often hunts by day.

NIGHTJAR
Grey-white camouflage plumage. Male has white spots near wing-tips. Long wings and tail. Wings held in deep V formation when gliding, which is interspersed with twisting zig-zag flight as it pursues insects. Often hovers, feeds mainly at night.

SHORT-EARED OWL
Buff-brown plumage with streaked breast. Long rounded wings with dark mark beneath. Short tail, short rounded head, yellow eyes. Longest-winged owl. Slow wavering flight when hunting. Will drop with raised wings, lifting quickly if there is no kill. 'Ears' are tufts of feather, not used for hearing. Regularly hunts in daylight.

SWIFT
Black-brown plumage except for white chin patch. Torpedo-shaped body. Long scythe-shaped wings curving backwards. Forked tail. Sexes alike.

SWALLOW
Steel blue upper, chestnut forehead and breast, light buff underparts. Deeply forked tail with streamers in adults. Female's streamers slightly shorter than male. Flies low over ground and skims across water.

female

male

HOUSE MARTIN
Small, blue-black above, white beneath, white rump. Forked tail becomes almost triangular when open. Wings appear curved when gliding.

SAND MARTIN
Small, plain brown above, white below, brown band across chest, tail short and slightly forked. Sexes alike.

WHIMBREL
Streaky buff-brown plumage (at a distance the tail looks white) distinguishable from Curlew by headmarkings of two dark stripes separated by pale streak. Female slightly larger than male. First indication of presence is usually its whistle. Wing-beat faster than Curlew. Fly singly or in small flocks.

GOLDEN PLOVER (summer)
Solid body, rounded head with long narrow pointed fast-beating wings, short tail. Black face and underparts with black-gold upper in summer. In winter black disappears, leaving underparts white with gold mottling. Sexes alike. Fly in tightly bunched flocks before spreading out to feed on landing.

KNOT (winter)
Solid body, short neck, short pale legs and straight black bill. Plumage grey above, paler in winter. Mottled black and chestnut above, russet underparts in summer, grey tail. Light rump and wing-bars show in flight. Long wings. Fly in huge massed flocks. A small flock consisting of 1,000 birds could be oval in shape, a large one could have 10,000 birds and be a narrower shape with trailing end.

DUNLIN
Small, brown-grey upper parts, lighter underparts in winter. Mottled grey upper, black under in summer, black patch under wings. At all ages and stages of plumage retains white bar on wings and white sides to tail. Skims in large flocks over water, identifiable by elongated shape. As flock wheels the whole cloud flickers grey and white.

REDSHANK
Long orange-red legs, broad white bars on trailing edges of wings, white triangle on rump. Grey brown with darker markings, light below. Appears darker in summer. Swift jerky flight, tilting from side to side. Sexes alike. Fly singly or in a small group.

CANADA GOOSE
Birds such as geese, ducks, gulls and cranes save some of the considerable energy used in flight, particularly on long journeys, flying in V formation. Each bird gets extra lift from the slip-stream created by the bird in front. Every now and then the leader drops back and another bird takes over the arduous task of pace-maker to the flock.

SWIFTS
Flying in a screaming party, this is particularly noticeable when they arrive in summer and when collecting together ready for migration in the autumn.

SWALLOWS, HOUSE MARTINS AND SAND MARTINS
showing their markings, wing and tail patterns.

Swallows and House Martins prepare for their migration flight

Take-off

To take-off, a bird must produce extra power in order to lift itself into the air. To do this the bird can either take-off into the wind like an aeroplane, or become airborne by jumping up and beating its wings backwards and forwards, and then continue normal flight by flapping its wings up and down. Another method is to take a running start and push itself strongly off the ground into the air. As you will see, birds have developed methods of take-off which suit their own particular needs.

The Redstart, like most land birds, crouches on its perch before springing into the air using the backwards and forwards method of beating its wings.

The Tufted Duck patters along the water flapping its wings to work up enough speed to fly into the wind, or is thrown upwards by an oncoming wave.

◄ **SWIFT**
Like the Swallow an excellent flyer, the Swift has poorly developed legs which prevent a good jump start, so it tends to fall forward from a high ledge.

BLACKBIRD ▶
Has stronger legs and can jump into the air from the ground.

TEAL
Like some ducks, the Teal can achieve near vertical take-off from the water as it is capable of enormous acceleration.

SWANS
Run along land or water surface, neck outstretched, wings thrashing. In a strong wind they may have to run one hundred metres before taking off.

MOORHENS
Like many swimming birds they patter laboriously across the water before they can take-off.

Landing

In order to land, birds must first of all reduce speed. This can be done in various ways. The simplest method for land birds is used by Woodpeckers. They swoop down below the chosen perch, then reduce speed by gliding up to the landing site.

A bird landing on the ground or on a perch reduces speed by bringing its body into a near vertical position to slow down, and spreads its wings and tail. As the body becomes more vertical, the danger of stalling is averted by spreading the alula feathers whilst back-pedalling with the wings. Finally, the legs are stretched out to absorb the impact of landing.

ROBIN
Typical landing posture.

GADWALL
In common with other surface feeding duck, Gadwalls stretch out their necks, taking the impact with their feet. Waterbirds do not need to be so accurate in their landing techniques as the water cushions the impact.

TUFTED DUCK
Ducks use their large feet as rudders when coming in to land. They back-pedal with their wings, spread their tails, and skid to a halt on the water surface on outstretched feet.

◀ **LAPWING**
The 'wings spread' posture of the Lapwing on landing which is typical of the braking effect needed to reduce speed and therefore impact on landing. The Lapwing in particular needs this steadying device, since part of its display consists of tumbling down from the sky, apparently out of control.

(Tufted Duck)

Beaks, feet and feeding habits

You can often tell what food a bird eats by looking at its beak and feet. In the following pages you will see how these are adapted for different kinds of feeding.

Feeding habits

Birds' beaks have to perform a wide variety of tasks, according to the environment in which they live and the type of food they eat. Seed and insect eaters tend to have small, sharp beaks, while waders have long, slim beaks for probing and spearing. Specialist beaks are found amongst woodpeckers, who need a sharp chisel for boring holes, and in seabirds who need to be able to hold slippery fish.

Feet are equally important in the search for food. Some birds scratch in the soil with long pointed claws; others, like waders, have wide-spread toes so that they can stand on soft mud without sinking in.

In every case, the type of beak and feet give clues to the bird's diet and method of feeding.

Seed-eaters

CROSSBILL
Seeds of pine, larch, spruce and conifers. Very occasionally fruit, weed seeds and insects. Seeds extracted with head laid sideways along cone.

HAWFINCH
Has plate of serrated ridges on roof of beak and lower jaw to give firm hold on large seeds, fruit stones, sometimes peas, haws and beech mast. Occasionally insects. Young birds have to eat soft seeds, until beak hardens.

GREENFINCH
Almost entirely seeds, wild fruit and berries. Visits bird-tables for sunflower seeds and peanuts. By active feeding can increase weight by about 10% to provide insulation against cold.

FIELDFARE
Wild fruit, garden berries, insects and small creatures such as earthworms, snails, beetles, slugs and caterpillars.

18

Insect eaters

ROBIN
Insects and larvae, fruit, seeds and earthworms.

GOLDCREST
Flies and other insects, spiders.

NIGHTJAR
Large flying insects chiefly caught at night. Mouth adapted to open both vertically and horizontally. 'Whiskers' protect eye from insect wings and legs. Pectinate claw enables bird to clean dust and insect debris from 'whiskers'.

SWIFT
Insects taken on wing, especially flies, small beetles, moths, which are collected into throat pouch, glued together with sticky saliva into a ball and fed to each young. Feet have all four small claws pointing forwards to assist grip on vertical surfaces.

COMMON TREECREEPER
Invertebrates, sometimes grain and weed seeds. Unlike woodpecker has three forward facing toes. Uses stiff pointed tail for support in similar manner.

19

Waders

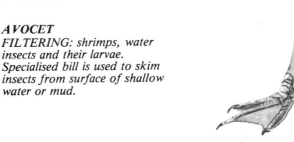

AVOCET
FILTERING: shrimps, water insects and their larvae. Specialised bill is used to skim insects from surface of shallow water or mud.

OYSTERCATCHER
PRISING: mussels, cockles, periwinkles and other molluscs, crabs, shrimps, inland worms and insects. Strong bill is used for striking into shell of prey and then prising it open.

WHIMBREL
PROBING: Inland, *insects and larvae, spiders, earthworms, snails, bilberries, crowberries. Coast, small crustacea, molluscs, marine worms. Long curved bill used for probing in sand and mud among shore pools and in shallow water.*

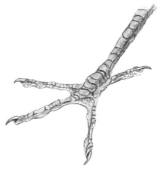

HERON
SPEARING: fish, water voles, beetles, frogs, moles and rats. Long, strong bill used for spearing its prey and picking flesh from bones.

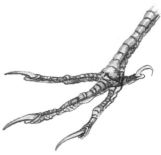

WATER RAIL
Insects, spiders, freshwater shrimps, earthworms, small fish, roots of grasses and watercress, seeds and berries. Have been seen carrying young and eggs from danger in their bills.

Geese and Swans

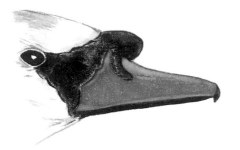

MUTE SWAN
Chiefly water vegetation, some small frogs, fish and insects. Black knob on base of bill is less prominent in female.

WHOOPER/BEWICK SWAN
Seeds and water plants. Whooper may also eat insects and molluscs.

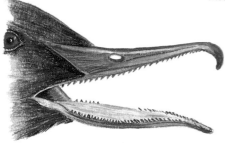

GOOSANDER
Small fish, shrimps and frogs, some caterpillars and other insects. Saw-edged bill makes it a very efficient angler.

PINK-FOOTED GOOSE
Grass, potatoes, grain and other crops. Webs between three toes.

BRENT GOOSE
Almost exclusively on eel grass in winter, will eat seaweed and mussels in summer. Will up-end like ducks to get at food.

GREAT-CRESTED GREBE
Small fish, molluscs, algae, weed and other vegetable matter. The expansible frill and raised ear-tufts identify. The paddle-shaped lobes on the toes have a similar effect to webbed feet in giving greater swimming power.

Sea and waterside birds

RED-THROATED DIVER
Many fish such as char, perch, herring, sprats, shrimps, mussels, and some insects. Sometimes found inland but prefers salt water.

COOT
Shoots of reeds, roots of water plants, corn and seeds, small fish, newts, tadpoles, dragonfly nymphs and other water insects, sometimes eggs and chicks of other birds. Will feed along stretches of coast when inland waters are frozen.

MOORHEN
Wild fruit and seeds, grain, water weed, worms, slugs, snails, insects and larvae, sometimes eggs and chicks of other birds.

EIDER DUCK
Mussels are their principal food, also whelks, cockles, and small crabs. Very little vegetable matter. Feet are used to create a hole in the mud which is then searched with the bill. When diving they use wings as well as feet.

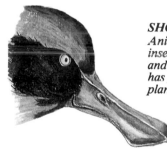

SHOVELER
Animal and vegetable food, freshwater insects and shellfish mixed with seeds, buds and leaves of water plants. Broad heavy bill has fine comb-like plates on edges to sieve plant and animal material.

SHELDUCK
Molluscs, small crabs and shrimps, insects, small amount of vegetable matter. Only male has distinctive red knob at base of bill. Food is obtained by up-ending in shallow water or foraging in mud.

MALLARD
Mainly seeds, buds and stems of water plants, some animal food. Webs between three toes increase area of foot, which is folded on forward stroke when swimming.

WIGEON

Mostly grasses, grain, also eel grass from mud-flats. Since little time is spent dabbling, they do not need the wide heavy bill of other ducks. Will graze near water's edge with other species. Use short wide bill to crop grass and plants using a shearing action.

SMEW

Variety of small fish, shrimps, snails and water beetles. Has tooth-like serrations along edges of bill to grip slippery fish.

BLACK-HEADED GULL

Scraps and offal in towns, elsewhere crabs, sand eels, moths, snails, earthworms and insects. Basically a scavenger and has developed the ability to snatch food found by Lapwings.

HERRING GULL

Offal, shellfish, eggs and chicks and fish. A scavenger and predator which has acquired skill for opening shellfish by dropping them from the air.

COMMON TERN

Small fish, especially sand eels, sometimes insects. When fishing they fly a metre or two above water and hover before diving, sometimes submerging completely.

FULMAR

Fish, whale or seal offal, also crustacea. The exact use of the complex beak structure is unknown, but it may help the bird to know how fast it is flying.

Sea and waterside birds

MANX SHEARWATER

Small fish such as herrings, sprats and pilchards. In daytime they gather in large rafts out to sea but come close inshore in the evenings. Much feeding done on the wing, skimming so close to the surface that the wings actually 'shear' the water, then hover before making a shallow dive.

SHAG

Fish, especially wrasse, blenny, goby, dragonet, garfish and sand eels, along rocky and open shores. Swims powerfully underwater propelled by feet which have webs between all four toes.

RINGED PLOVER

Molluscs, crustacea, many types of insect, worms and some vegetable matter. Prey is driven to surface by rapid paddling on wet sand with one foot.

GANNET

Fish, edible offal. Skull is specially strengthened to withstand the impact of water when dive-bombing their catch from heights of up to thirty metres.

CORMORANT

Chiefly flat fish, also wrasse, sand eels, sticklebacks, occasionally crabs. Can dive for 20–30 seconds to a depth of ten metres. Big fish are brought to the surface before being swallowed.

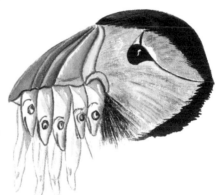

PUFFIN

Marine organisms including molluscs and fish. Sand eels can be collected neatly together in specially hinged beak. Loose fold of orange lip allows upper and lower half of bill to close parallel, gripping the eels firmly along whole length of bill.

Birds of prey

GOLDEN EAGLE
Blue hares, grouse, ptarmigan and carrion. Powerful talons are used for perching and seizing and carrying prey.

BARN OWL
Rodents, small birds, beetles, frogs, sometimes fish and bats. Long spindly legs, fairly hairy. Exceptionally long beak for an owl.

TAWNY OWL
Small mammals, some birds, occasionally fish and frogs, molluscs, worms and insects. Flexible neck allows it to turn its head almost full circle. Short feathered legs and toes.

SPARROWHAWK
Mainly small birds such as sparrows and finches, occasionally the larger female kills birds as big as pigeons. Some mice, voles and young rabbits, occasionally insects. Long unfeathered legs.

OSPREY
Almost entirely fish, mainly pike and trout. Scales on footpads have small spines for grasping and carrying slippery fish.

Feet for climbing and perching

GREAT SPOTTED WOODPECKER
Strong claws with two backwards facing toes to give good grip whilst climbing and boring holes.

NUTHATCH
Same climbing function as Woodpecker but different toe formation, three forward-facing.

MEADOW PIPIT
Long legs and long hind claw gives bird good balance, making it a strong walker.

CUCKOO
Perching bird with two front and two back facing toes.

PARTRIDGE
Strong foot with shortened hind toe reduces area of foot touching the ground, gives the bird greater speed.

NESTS

◀GOLDCREST
Smallest British breeding bird. Both sexes build intricate hammock of moss and spiders' webs, lined with feathers, attached by 'handles' to branches, favouring conifers, or in creeper near trunk of tree. Seven to ten white or pale buff eggs. April–June.

BLACKBIRD ▶
Bulky, cup-shaped nest of stems, grasses and moss, plastered and lined with mud and dried grass, built mainly by female. Usually in bush or ivy against a wall, also on buildings and in trees. Three to five eggs, greenish-blue in colour with dark markings. Late March–July.

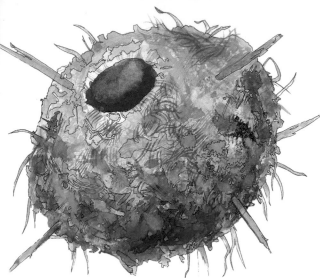

LONG-TAILED TIT
Both sexes build oval-shaped nest, from inside, of cobwebs, moss and hair, the feather lining alone may need over 2,000 journeys. Normally decorated with lichens, but in polluted areas around cities this may be replaced by paper or even polystyrene. Usually placed low in gorse or hawthorn. Eight to twelve eggs, white with reddish markings. April–May.

SONG THRUSH ▶
Female builds cup-shaped nest of twigs, grass and moss plastered with mud, dung and saliva. Distinguishable from Blackbird's nest by hard lining. Usually in bushes or trees up to about eight metres from ground, also amongst creepers on banks and walls. Three to five blue eggs, lightly marked. Late March–July.

◀ REED WARBLER
Deep cylindrical cup, built chiefly by female, attached to reeds at height of about one metre, around several stems of reeds; woven with grass, stems and flower heads, lined with grass, wool and feathers. Nearly always in reedbeds near water. Four to five eggs, greenish white with dark markings. May–August.

DIPPER ▶
Bulky, dome-shaped nest built by both sexes working from the inside, made of moss and lined with dried leaves. Built a little above fast flowing water, mainly in hilly districts, in crevices or on ledges, often under bridges or behind waterfalls. When the nest is built in this position, the birds fly through the cascading water. Approximately five eggs, dull white. Late February–June.

◄ CORMORANT

Nest built by both sexes consists of mound of seaweed, sticks and local vegetation along ledges on rocky coasts and occasionally on inland cliffs near water. Sometimes old nests of other species built in trees are used. Three to five pale blue eggs with chalky markings. April–August.

GANNET ►

Mound of seaweed and local vegetation about sixty centimetres high, usually on steep cliffs. Materials gathered by both sexes before eggs are laid, thereafter only by male. One egg, chalky white, soon becomes stained. April–August.

◄ LITTLE GREBE

Floating mound of water plants and leaves built by both sexes, either onto submerged spit, or anchored by surrounding vegetation. Usually four to six white eggs which soon become stained. April–July.

GREAT-CRESTED GREBE ►

Floating tangle of water weeds, reeds and rushes anchored to submerged spit or surrounding plants; built by both sexes. When leaving nest, the bird covers eggs with weeds if there is time. Nest has been seen built on an artificial raft.

◀ NIGHTJAR

Very simple nest, usually just a scrape in the ground often amongst dry bracken with a few dead sticks scattered near by. Usually two grey-white marbled eggs. May–August.

LITTLE RINGED PLOVER ▶

Female selects one of several simple scrapes made in bare ground; inland on gravel and shingle banks, dried mud or flat waste ground, or on sandy coasts. May line it with pebbles and local vegetation. Usually four greyish buff eggs with dark markings, smaller than Ringed Plover. Late April–July.

◀ WOODCOCK

Nest is a scrape in open woods or rough ground, lined with plenty of dead leaves, often by a tree. Four grey-white to light brown eggs with dark markings. March–July.

LAPWING ▶

Male makes several scrapes in ploughed field or rough grassland, female lines one with pieces of local vegetation. Usually four eggs, buff to dark brown with dark markings. Late March–June.

◀ WOODPECKER

Hole made in mature tree by both sexes in deciduous woods, large gardens or occasionally in built-up areas. Circular to oval entrance hole. No nesting material used, but wood chips cushion eggs at bottom of shaft 30–60cm deep. Five to seven eggs, white. April–June. Woodpecker nest sites may be used by different species in following seasons, enlarging or blocking up entrance holes as necessary.

Birds of Gardens and Woods

Male Blackbird

Female Blackbird

Blackbird
Family Thrushes

The Blackbird is almost as well known as the Robin; or, at least, the male is, for he is the one with the sooty black plumage and bright orange-yellow bill. The female blackbird is sometimes confused with the Song Thrush as she is brownish and her breast, especially in the first year, is mottled.

The Blackbird has a tuneful, fluting song and sometimes copies human music. When it is alarmed, it gives a hysterical cackle and sounds like a different bird.

Its food consists of fruit, seeds, insects and worms; you may have seen it pulling worms out of the lawn in your garden or local park. It is a common visitor to bird-tables where it enjoys fat, dried fruit and cake crumbs.

The Blackbird's breeding season extends from March to July and it can have two or three broods and sometimes four. The nest is built by the hen and consists of mud, moss, and grass; sometimes the cock bird helps. There are usually four to five eggs.

Blackbirds are with us all the year round and in winter some are visitors from Europe. They are found all over Britain and number about seven million pairs.

Male Blackcap

Blackcap
Family Warblers

The Blackcap is a summer visitor mainly from Southern Europe and North Africa. It arrives in Britain usually between the second week of April and the end of May. It is a greyish-brown bird and the male has the black cap; the female, a brown one.

The sweet song is similar to that of the Garden Warbler, but richer. The Blackcap is fairly easy to see as it often sings from open trees; its food consists of insects, berries and fruit.

Blackcaps nest usually in bushes or hedges in woodland and the hen does most of the building using grass and roots. There are normally five eggs.

By October these charming little birds leave us, but a few Blackcaps spend the winter in Britain. These are probably visitors from Europe.

Female Blackcap

Blue Tit
Family Titmice

The Blue Tit is a great garden bird-table favourite; its acrobatics are always a delight to watch. It is the most common member of the Tit family and never seems to tire of eating peanuts which are a good food in winter because of the fat content. During the breeding season however peanuts taken by the parents to the nest can kill the nestlings which need their natural food of insects and particularly caterpillars.

The Blue Tit's bright blue cap, wings and tail make it easy to identify. The underparts are yellow and there may be a narrow black line down the breast. Another black line edges the white cheeks, passing through the eye and giving the bird what look rather like spectacles. The call is 'tsee-tsee-tsee'.

Blue Tits nest in holes, and sometimes in most unlikely ones such as street lamp standards and letter-boxes. The nest is of moss and grass, lined with hair, wool and feathers. If you have some trees and shrubs in the garden, where the parent birds can find plenty of caterpillars, it is a good idea to put up a nesting box. The eggs can number from seven to fourteen or even more and are white, speckled with brown.

Blue Tits remain in Britain all the year round and number about five million pairs.

Male Brambling

Female Brambling

Brambling
Family Finches

The Brambling is a winter visitor from Northern Europe and Asia, although there is one definite breeding record in Scotland.

They are not common although they may sometimes be overlooked when feeding on the ground with Chaffinches. The differences are that the cock Brambling does not have the Chaffinch's white shoulder patch and its breast is not pink but orange. It also has a distinctive white patch above the base of the tail; an orange shoulder patch and a white wing bar.

As the winter turns to spring, some may show the black hood of their summer plumage. The females are very similar to chaffinch females in appearance, but have the white rump which is the most noticeable difference.

Bramblings eat seeds, beechmast, wheat and berries. They arrive in Britain from the end of September and leave again from March to the first half of May.

Bullfinch
Family Finches

The Bullfinch is one of our most colourful and handsome birds, but is unpopular with fruit growers and gardeners because it picks buds off fruit trees and ornamental shrubs in spring. Bullfinches turn to fruit buds when there are no seeds on the ash trees, which they prefer. Some gardeners are prepared to forgive the loss of a few buds for the beautiful colouring of the robbers.

The male has a black cap and a deep rose-pink breast. Its back is blue-grey and it has a white rump. The female also has a black cap but is less brightly coloured.

The song of the Bullfinch, when compared with its stout form and bright colours sounds like 'oh dear – dear me' – as if the bird were ashamed of its bad reputation. The call note is a sad 'den' but is rarely heard.

Its nest made of twigs and moss and dark-coloured roots may be found in gardens and hedges. There are four to five eggs. Both parents feed the chicks by 'regurgitation' which means that they swallow the food and partly digest it in their crops, before returning it and pumping it into the throats of the young.

Male Bullfinch

Female Bullfinch

Chaffinch
Family Finches

Not many birds have calls which can be imitated successfully by human words, but the 'pink' call of the Chaffinch is one of them. It also describes the bird's appearance, as the breast and cheeks of the adult male are pinkish-brown and the underparts pink. The female is a pale brown; lighter underneath. Chaffinches have a tripping walk or hop, bobbing their heads like mechanical toys, and a dipping, undulating flight.

The song consists of several descending notes, ending in a flourish, which may differ from place to place. Chaffinches are mainly seed-eaters. Other vegetable matter taken includes fruit and some corn. They also destroy many insects.

The nest is beautifully made, and often placed in the fork of a branch and then decorated with lichen. It is made of grass, roots and moss, lined with hair. There are usually four to five eggs. Chaffinches are present all the year in the British Isles. They have suffered a decline, perhaps because of toxic seed dressings, but remain one of Britain's commonest birds, with a breeding population of seven million pairs.

Male Chaffinch

Female Chaffinch

34

Chiffchaff
Family Warblers

As one of the earliest of our summer visitors, the Chiffchaff's song is eagerly awaited each year: it sounds like its name – 'Chiff-chaff' – repeated time after time. It is not hard to recognise the Chiffchaff as it moves about almost continually singing among the leaves. If it isn't singing then identification is almost impossible, so closely does it resemble the Willow Warbler.

Like other warblers, the Chiffchaff feeds on insects, small spiders and their eggs. The nest is a round ball of moss, leaves and stalks lined with feathers and is built in brambles and thick vegetation, usually off the ground. It has a side entrance and is built by the hen only. There are normally six eggs.

Chiffchaffs come to us from the Mediterranean and North Africa in March and usually leave in August, but a few spend the winter here.

Coal Tit
Family Titmice

Coal Tits, if there were more of them, would probably be as popular as Blue Tits at the bird-table. They are even more interesting to watch, as they do not eat their food on the spot but carry it away to hide for future use. The Coal Tits may appear to be numerous, but careful watching shows that it is probably only one or two pairs keeping up a shuttle service.

The Coal Tit is slightly smaller than the Blue Tit. Its face pattern is similar to that of the larger Great Tit but it has a large distinctive white patch on the nape of the neck.

Coal Tits principally eat insects, but also spiders, weed seeds, the kernels of nuts, beechmast and conifer seeds. They come to the bird-table for nuts and fat.

The nest which is of moss with a layer of hair, is in a hole near the ground in a bank or a tree or an old stump. There are from seven to eleven eggs.

The Coal Tit is present all the year in the British Isles, only moving locally between winter and summer. There are about one million breeding pairs.

35

Collared Dove
Family Pigeons and Doves

This is a highly successful newcomer. It has spread from Asia right across Europe over the past fifty years and now breeds in all counties of the British Isles. Yet the first breeding record ever was in Norfolk in 1955. Now its rather melancholy call of 'coo-cooo-cuk' can be heard throughout the land.

The Collared Dove is quite easy to identify by its colouring which is grey-brown above and pinkish-grey below. Note the black half collar. The tail is long and in flight shows a distinct white tip.

It feeds on grain and so is often seen near poultry farms. Farmers and market gardeners regard it as a pest.

The nest is made of twigs and stems and usually placed fairly high up in a tree or on the ledge of a building. There are two eggs. Like the rest of the Pigeon family, Collared Doves feed their young on a special product of their crops called 'pigeon milk'.

They are present all the year and are still expanding their range to the north-west.

Crested Tit
Family Titmice

Crested Tits are the second smallest of the family after the Coal Tit. In Britain they are only seen in the central Highlands of Scotland. Their stronghold is in the Spey valley where there are remnants of the ancient Caledonian forest. They are birds of the pinewoods and eat the insects from the pines; they also eat conifer seeds and juniper berries. With the planting of new forests this engaging little bird is slowly increasing its range.

There is no identification problem – the pointed, black and white crest is clear and the sexes are alike. It is fairly silent but has a soft call 'tsi-tsi-tsi' and a churr or trill.

The nest, of moss lined with hair, is in a hole which may be dug out by the female in a rotten tree stump or sometimes natural holes are used in a tree or post. There are five to six eggs.

Crested Tits are present all the year.

Collared Dove

Crossbill
Family Finches

This is a bird with a specially adapted crossed beak – to prise open pine and spruce cones. Another unusual feature of the Crossbill is the invasions which occur from time to time, when large numbers reach the British Isles from Scandinavia. The reason is connected with the size of the crops of conifer seed in their country of origin. After the breeding season, many of the Crossbills leave in search of food and continue moving west until it is found. On arrival here they can be seen moving sideways along the branches like miniature parrots.

Two races of Crossbills exist in the British Isles – the Common and the Scottish – although neither of them is really common. The adult males are brick-red and the females yellowish-green. As they fly they call a loud 'jip, jip'. The main difference is that the Scottish Crossbill has a stouter bill.

The nest of pine twigs, grasses and wool is built by the hen. There are usually four eggs. Both parents feed the chicks by regurgitation (*see* Bullfinch). They breed mainly in the central Highlands of Scotland, East Anglia and the New Forest. 'Invasions' occur from late summer onwards when their food supply of fir cones fails in Scandinavia.

Crested Tit

Scottish Crossbills (Male left, Female right)

Common Male Crossbill

Common Female Crossbill

Cuckoo
Family Cuckoos

◀ The Cuckoo's two hollow-sounding notes in spring and its habit of laying eggs in the nests of other birds, make it of especial interest and curiosity. With its blue-grey upperparts and whitish underparts barred with dark grey, the bird in flight is sometimes mistaken for a male Sparrowhawk, but the Cuckoo has a white tip to its long tail, and flies with rapid, shallow wing beats.

Cuckoos feed mainly on insects. They also eat caterpillars, including the hairy ones which most birds ignore.

After selecting a nest, the Cuckoo takes only eleven seconds to lay her egg and make off with one of the host bird's eggs in her bill. In all, she may lay up to twelve or thirteen eggs, like tiny time-bombs, in the nests of other unsuspecting birds in her territory. The Cuckoo's egg usually hatches first and the fledgling promptly proceeds to heave all the other eggs or chicks out of the nest. The foster-parents then have to work non-stop to provide the fat changeling with food.

Cuckoos are summer visitors to the British Isles from Central and South Africa and Southern Arabia, arriving in April. The adults leave in July, and the juveniles in August.

Dunnock with young

Dunnock
Family Accentors

This bird is sometimes called a 'Hedge Sparrow' although it has no relationship with sparrows at all. The old country name of Dunnock is a much better one for it. A close look shows that it has an insect-eater's thin beak rather than the thick grain-eater's beak of a sparrow.

It is rather inconspicuous in a sober brown suit with its head and neck blue-grey, less so in the female. The thin bill is black. Another identification feature is the bird's habit of flicking its wings rapidly. The Dunnock's song, like its appearance, is quiet and demure, a thin jingle. Dunnocks eat quantities of insects in summer, although their diet in winter is almost entirely of weed seeds.

The nest is built in hedges and evergreens, in ivy and on banks. It is built, by the hen alone, of twigs, moss, leaves and roots, lined with moss, hair or wool. There are usually four to five eggs.

The Dunnock is a partial migrant, moving southwards in the latter half of September in some years. There are about five million pairs in Britain and Ireland.

Garden Warbler
Family Warblers

A summer visitor whose fame rests with its song. It is a small, plump, brown bird with paler underparts, and this lack of distinguishing marks means that it is often best identified by its song. Unfortunately this is very like that of the Blackcap so that even experienced ornithologists cannot always be one hundred per cent sure. The song has the same mellow quality as the Blackcap's, but is quieter and the bird sings from undergrowth.

The Garden Warbler is not aptly named as it prefers thick scrub and is more likely to be seen and heard on the edge of woodland than in an ordinary garden. The nest is made of dry grass and moss and placed low down. Both sexes help to build it and take turns to sit on the four to five eggs. The young are fed on insects but the parents also eat spiders, worms, fruit and berries.

Garden Warblers arrive from Central and Southern Africa about mid-April and some may remain until October, although their singing ends in mid-July. They are rare in Ireland and Northern Scotland.

Garden Warbler

Goldcrest at nest

Goldcrest
Family Goldcrests or Kinglets

With the Firecrest the Goldcrest is our smallest bird at less than eight centimetres long. Five of them would weigh only 28 grams or 1 ounce. It lives mainly in the treetops, but if seen closely can be identified by its greenish colour and particularly by the bright orange or yellow crown with a black border. The song is quite different from that of any other British bird, being a thin, high-pitched rhythmic sound. Its food consists of insects and spiders.

The nest is an intricate structure of moss, interwoven with spiders' webs and lined with feathers. It is often found in a conifer, suspended near the end of a branch, and may be at any height up to fifteen metres. Both sexes build the nest but incubation is by the hen. There are normally two broods of ten young.

Goldcrests suffer big losses in hard winters but are able to recover their numbers rapidly by raising large families. They have also benefited from the planting of conifer trees. Although resident all the year, there are local movements south in winter.

Goldfinch
Family Finches

It is a delightful sight when a family party or 'charm' of these colourful little birds descends like golden rain on the thistle seeds they love.

We are fortunate that we can still see these birds today because by the end of the last century they had become very rare as they were trapped for the cage-bird trade. Luckily, the Society for the Protection of Birds was formed in 1891 and soon helped to make the trapping of songbirds illegal.

Their flight is buoyant and they constantly give bell-like, tinkling calls. They feed mainly on seed but insects are taken too.

The female builds the nest in gardens and orchards; sometimes in ornamental conifers. It is neatly made of moss, lichens and grass, with a lining of wool. The hen does all the incubation. When the five or six eggs hatch after twelve or thirteen days the young are fed by regurgitation (*see* Bullfinch). There are usually two broods. The Goldfinch is present all the year but there are local flock movements. It is rare in Northern Scotland.

Male Great Spotted Woodpecker

Female Great Spotted Woodpecker

Great Spotted Woodpecker
Family Woodpeckers

This is the second largest of our woodpeckers being about twenty three centimetres long. Its colouring is striking; only the male has the crimson patch at the back of the head. The young birds have crimson on the entire crown.

The Great Spotted is the most common of the three British woodpeckers and breeds in almost every mainland county. They have even spread to town parks and in some districts often visit garden bird-tables — especially when there is a supply of suet. Walking through woodland you are more likely to hear its drumming sound than to see the bird. Drumming has much the same purpose as bird song; it attracts a female and warns off other males. Dry branches are used near the tops of trees. The bird strikes about ten times per second and the sound can carry nearly half a kilometre.

You may also hear its call — a loud 'tchick' — and then see its deeply dipping flight. They nest in holes which they bore in old trees. There are from four to seven eggs. The Great Spotted Woodpecker is present all the year. The bird is increasing in numbers, possibly helped by the plentiful supply of insects in elms dead from Dutch elm disease.

Great Tit
Family Titmice

Great and Blue Tits are by far the most common of the titmouse family and they are star-turns at bird-tables. The word titmouse has nothing to do with small rodents, but derives from the Old English word 'mase' meaning a small bird.

The Great Tit is the largest of the family, being sixteen centimetres long, and is the only one with a broad black band down its middle. This black band is broader in the male than in the female. It also has a whitish area at the back of the crown but not a distinct white patch like the Coal Tit. It feeds on insects, spiders, fruit and nuts.

It has an astonishing variety of calls but the best known is the two note sound 'tea-cher, tea-cher', like a cheerful hammering, which is one of the most insistent sounds of spring.

Great Tits nest in a hole in a tree or wall and frequently in nest boxes. The nests are built of moss and lined with hair or down. There are from five to eleven eggs and normally there is one brood only. Great Tits are present all the year round.

Male Greenfinch

Female Greenfinch

Greenfinch
Family Finches

The old country name for this bird is Green Linnet but Greenfinch is now its accepted common name. It is a thick billed seed-eater and a great frequenter of bird-tables. The male has the more splendid plumage with his olive-green colour and yellow wing-bars and tail-sides.

In winter they sometimes leave the safety of the garden and join with flocks of other finches or buntings feeding on stubble. They have a distinctive bounding flight when disturbed.

The Greenfinch has a variety of calls but the most distinctive can be heard in the sweltering heat of a mid-summer day – an unmistakable drowsy drawn-out note which sounds like 'bree-ee-eeze'.

The nest of twigs and moss lined with hair is built in bushes, trees or hedges. Only the hen sits on the four to six eggs and she is fed on the nest by the male. Both sexes feed the chicks by regurgitation (*see* Bullfinch). Normally there are two broods and occasionally three. The Greenfinch is present all the year and some foreign birds winter in Britain.

Green Woodpecker
Family Woodpeckers

The Green Woodpecker is the largest of the three British woodpeckers; it is also the most brightly coloured. The difference in appearance between the sexes is that the male has a vivid red stripe under the eye – in the female it is black. Both have a bright yellow rump which shows clearly in flight.

You are more likely to see this bird on the ground than in trees, as it is expert at raiding ants' nests with its long sticky-ended tongue.

As with all our woodpeckers, two toes point to the front and two back, which makes climbing trees easier.

The Green Woodpecker's loud ringing call sounds like a mad laugh and accounts for its country name of Yaffle. Rainbird is another of its names, probably because its laugh is heard most frequently in the showery month of April.

Both sexes bore the nesting hole in a tree; there are from five to seven eggs and the young are fed by regurgitation (*see* Bullfinch).

Green Woodpeckers are present all the year in England and Wales.

Male Green Woodpecker

cherry stone to reach the soft kernel although a crushing force of between twenty seven and forty three kilograms is needed to fracture the shell. Apart from cracking fruit stones, it also likes haws, beech mast and garden peas.

The song is seldom heard and nondescript. Hawfinches breed in woods, parks, big gardens and orchards: their nests are built of twigs, roots and lichens and lined with hair. There is one brood, occasionally two, and there are usually four to six eggs. The birds are present all the year in most of Britain, but are not found in Ireland and rarely in Scotland.

Hawfinch
Family Finches

This is the largest of the British finches. It is a secretive, wary bird and difficult to see as it likes to perch among the tops of tall trees. The flight is high and deeply bounding. If seen on the ground, it hops awkwardly and appears top-heavy with its big head and short tail.

The Hawfinch's principal feature is its massive bill which is steel blue in summer, yellow in winter. The bill extends the line of the head like the point of a bullet. It is powerful enough to crack open a

House Martin
Family Swallows

The House Martin is sometimes confused with the Swallow but it is slightly smaller and has a conspicuous white rump. Its other distinguishing features are white underparts feathered right down to the toes and a less deeply forked tail than the Swallow, without the long streamers.

House Martins also differ from Swallows in their custom of nesting in colonies, especially in the country. The nests of mud are marvels of architectural and plastering skill. They are a familiar sight under the eaves of houses and other buildings or they may be placed under a bridge, in caves or on a cliff. There must always be water nearby to provide the mud that is their building material. ▼

One of the pleasing things about having House Martins under the eaves is the companionable bubbling sound of their warbling. There are usually four to five eggs and two or sometimes three broods. When there are young in the nest there is ceaseless activity as both parents search for food, which includes almost every type of flying insect.

House Martins are summer visitors from South Africa. They arrive in Britain during April and start to leave during August.

Male House Sparrow

House Sparrow
Family Sparrows

Sparrows are thought to be related to African Weaver-birds and to have spread to Europe when primitive people began to cultivate crops. They are still largely confined to human dwellings, where as seed-eaters they find easy pickings and good lodgings.

In town a House Sparrow looks a drab little bird but seen in clean country air he is quite smart with a grey crown, chestnut on the back of the neck, a black throat and white cheeks. The hen is brown with a streaked back.

Autumn is the one time when the House Sparrow leaves buildings and moves to farmland to feed on the grain. The bird cannot be said to have a song but just a number of chirpings and cheepings.

Female House Sparrow

The breeding season usually begins in May, although eggs may be found at almost any time of year. The nest is often just an untidy mess of straw and rubbish straggling from a drainpipe or placed in some crevice on the outside of a house, but when built in a bush it is neat and domed with a side entrance. There are three to five eggs and often three broods are raised.

House Sparrows are present all the year round.

Jackdaw
Family Crows

Jackdaws are easily distinguishable from other crows by their smaller size and grey on the back and sides of the head. Their main call is a sharp 'chack'.

They are often seen on sea cliffs, around church towers, ruins or old trees. Jackdaws are great robbers and pick up all sorts of little objects they can't eat and then hide them. Their food consists mainly of insects but they also take young birds and eggs. They will in fact eat almost anything including corn, potatoes, fruit, berries and nuts.

They are sociable birds and nest in colonies. Sometimes they pluck wool from the backs of

sheep and use it for lining their nests, which are built of twigs. There are three to six eggs. The hen sits and is fed by the male. The eggs hatch after eighteen days and the young are fed by both parents. The chicks thrust their heads into the parents' mouths and take the food from their throat pouches.

Jackdaws are present all the year round.

Jay
Family Crows

The Jay is one of our most brightly coloured birds. It is more of a woodland bird than any other British crow. Before you see it, you may hear its characteristic harsh cry, then catch a glimpse of a pinkish brown bird and a flash of white rump and black tail. In recent years they moved into London's parks and many a town-dweller must have been inspired to take an interest in birdlife by the first sight of an exotic Jay.

In autumn Jays pluck acorns and bury them in order to have a store of food available in hard weather. Some are forgotten and so help the spread of many oak trees.

Apart from acorns, they also take eggs, young birds, insects, and some peas, potatoes, corn and berries.

The nest which consists of twigs and earth lined with roots is built by both sexes and there are three to six eggs. There is only one brood.

Jays are present all the year but are not found in Northern Scotland.

Kestrel
Family Falcons

Kestrels are easily the best known of our birds of prey. They have become a great attraction for drivers on motorways and it is no wonder that this small falcon was chosen as the emblem for the Young Ornithologists' Club of the RSPB.

Motorway verges and embankments are left undisturbed, so there is an abundance of voles and other small mammals and insects on which the bird feeds. Its hovering flight is most distinctive as it heads into the wind and holds its position by flying at the same speed as the wind. The Kestrel's call is a shrill 'kee-kee-kee'. Both sexes have brownish plumage. The male has a grey head and tail.

Kestrels began to spread into the cities in the 1930s. High buildings provide nesting sites and sparrows are plentiful as prey. In the country they may be seen on moors, coasts, farmland and in open woodland. The birds are a friend to the farmer because they control the mice and rats.

They do not build nests of their own but make use of ledges on cliffs or high buildings, a hole in a tree or sometimes the abandoned nests of crows or other birds. There are three to five eggs.

Kestrels are present all the year.

Lesser Spotted Woodpecker
Family Woodpeckers

This is a bird which is very shy and not easy to see, unless you are lucky enough to be looking out of your window when one visits your garden. They are small too, being the smallest European woodpecker, only fourteen centimetres long, the size of a Greenfinch. Unlike the Greater Spotted Woodpecker (twenty three centimetres long) the Lesser has no red under the tail and its back is barred black and white. The male has a crimson crown; on the female it is white.

This little woodpecker also drums but comparatively softly. Its call is a loud 'pee-pee-pee-pee'.

Lesser Spotted Woodpeckers eat mainly the larvae of insects which live in wood. They also eat other insects and spiders.

Their breeding season is usually from the middle of May and the nesting hole, which is bored by both sexes, is in rotten wood. There is no nest material except a few chips of wood; the eggs are four to six in number. There is only one brood.

Lesser Spotted Woodpeckers are present in England and Wales all the year.

Long-eared Owl
Family Owls

The 'ears' have nothing to do with hearing, but are simply long tufts of feathers. It is a very difficult bird to see as it hunts for small mammals, birds and insects by night and spends the day roosting, flattened against the trunk of a tree, so that it is almost invisible.

This mysterious owl makes a curious and eerie range of sounds. The principal note is a long-drawn 'oo-oo-oo' which is more like a moan than a hoot and can be heard at a distance of over half a kilometre. In courtship the male displays to the female by clapping its wings together and jumping in the air. When angry it hisses and snaps and in the breeding season makes a call like a bark.

Long-eared owls normally nest in pinewoods using the old nests of crows or other birds, but may sometimes be found in copses or in clumps of trees in large gardens. Four to six white eggs are laid and there is usually only one brood.

Long-eared Owls are present all the year and the east coast of Britain may be visited in autumn and spring by a few passage migrants.

45

Long-tailed Tits
Family Titmice

If it weren't for its tail which is longer than its body, this little bird would be Britain's smallest. Like all the members of its family it is extremely active and acrobatic and the delicate pink, black and white plumage is of great beauty. It feeds on insects, seeds and spiders.

Perhaps its greatest distinction is that it builds one of the most marvellous nests of any British bird. The nest is domed and the small entrance-hole is near the top. It is made of cobwebs, moss, lichens, hair and above all, feathers. These are used as a soft lining and as many as two thousand feathers may be used. The entrance is so tiny that the parent birds have to fold their tails over their heads when they go inside. There are eight to twelve eggs and normally only one brood.

In winter they form family flocks and roam through high woodland making their characteristic call 'see-see-see'.

Long-tailed Tits are present all the year. ▼

◀ Magpie
Family Crows

At a distance Magpies may appear black and white, but close to, the bird is seen to have a glossy sheen of blue, green, or purple. The tail is long and tapering and when you see a Magpie in dipping flight with rounded wings, it seems to have quite a job pulling the long tail after it. It also has an awkward way of walking with occasional sideways hops. The Magpie feeds on insects, small mammals, eggs, worms and some vegetable matter.

Like all crows, the Magpie is a hoarder and in addition to food will hide almost any coloured object it fancies. The main call is a harsh cackle and they often chatter as they chase each other about in the branches. In late winter or early spring large excited gatherings of the birds take place, but the reason for these parties is not known.

Of recent years Magpies have spread into towns and have colonised several city parks.

The nest is large, domed and made of sticks, usually in a tall tree or thorny bush. There is one clutch of four to seven eggs.

The Magpie is present all the year.

Marsh Tit
Family Titmice

This member of the tit family looks almost exactly the same as its relation the Willow Tit. Even experts sometimes have difficulty in distinguishing them. There are minor differences in plumage: the Marsh Tit has a glossy black crown which does not extend far down the nape, while that of the Willow Tit is dull and extends well down the nape.

The best way to distinguish them is by their calls: the Marsh Tit has a soft 'pitchew' call, while the Willow's is a grating, low-pitched 'chay' or a 'zi-zurr-zurr-zurr' note. ▶

Another confusion is that the Marsh is not found in marshes nor the Willow in willow trees. They both frequent damp woodland and seldom come to bird-tables. Marsh Tits feed on insects, seeds, berries and nuts.

They nest in holes in trees or stone walls and the nest has a foundation of moss with a lining of hair and sometimes rabbit's fur. There are usually six to eight eggs.

Marsh Tits are present all the year but are not found in Ireland or Scotland.

Mistle Thrush

Mistle Thrush
Family Thrushes

This is a larger and more impressive bird than the Song Thrush. It can be distinguished by its grey-brown upperparts and bigger, rounder spots.

Another difference is that in flight it shows white patches under the wing.

Its name is said to refer to its liking for mistletoe berries. Another name for it is 'Storm Cock' as it will sing from the topmost branches of a tall tree in a winter gale.

In the autumn Mistle Thrushes take to open country in family flocks – the young have yellow on the upper parts and white flecks. The flight call is a harsh 'churring' sound, like the rattle made by a piece of wood when drawn across the teeth of a coarse comb; the same sound is made louder for the alarm note.

They feed mostly on the ground and have a more upright stance than the Song Thrush. Their food consists of fruit and berries, also worms, snails, insects and spiders.

The nest is often high up and in the fork of a tree; it is made of grass, moss and earth, lined with grasses. There are usually four eggs. The Mistle Thrush is present all the year.

Nightingale
Family Thrushes

Not everybody realises that the Nightingale sings as much in the daytime as at night. The cock birds arrive from Africa in mid-April and it is they who are the singers. The females arrive about ten days later.

The song of the Nightingale is incomparable. There is none other with such richness, variety and vigour. The two outstanding phrases are repetitions of one note. One is a deep, unforgettable throbbing sound, the other a long drawn-out plaintive piping note.

Its fame is entirely due to the song, as in appearance it is quite undistinguished – just a little brown bird with a reddish-brown tail and whitish-brown underparts. It feeds on worms and insects. The Nightingale is not an easy bird to see as it conceals itself in tangled greenery and builds its nest of leaves and grasses close to the ground in thick undergrowth. There are usually four or five eggs.

In the breeding season the bird can become quite aggressive in defence of its young and then has a harsh, scolding alarm note quite unlike the beauty of its song.

Nightingales are summer visitors to England departing in August and September. They can be seen mainly south and east of a line from the Severn to the Humber, and very rarely in South Wales.

Nuthatch
Family Nuthatches　▲

The Nuthatch might be mistaken for a mouse as it scuttles up or down the trunk of a tree. Seen closer it is a colourful, stubby little bird. Note the pick-axe bill which makes it much respected at bird-tables, when it arrives in direct flight like a tiny aerial torpedo and may land any way up. Suet, and of course nuts, it finds irresistible.

In the woods the Nuthatch is difficult to spot. Listen first for its clear, cheerful, whistling notes and then home-in on the little slate-blue bird climbing in short jerks in constant search of insects behind the bark of trees. It also wedges nuts in bark and cracks them open with its bill.

The Nuthatch is a hole-nesting bird. It chooses a suitable hole usually in a tree and then proceeds to make the entrance smaller by plastering it with mud. This often prevents the nest being taken over by other birds, especially Starlings. The nest is built from pieces of bark: there are usually six to eleven eggs.

The Nuthatch is present all the year, but does not occur in Ireland.

Pied Flycatcher
Family Flycatchers

To see this handsome little bird you would have to visit hill-side woods of oak or ash by fast-flowing streams. This greatly limits its breeding area and it is mostly confined to Wales, and bordering English counties, parts of the Pennines, the Lake District, and some parts of Scotland.

It is a hole-nester and depends on the availability of nesting holes in trees, walls, or nest boxes near water. As these are in short supply, the RSPB has provided numerous nesting boxes on its Welsh reserves.

The Pied Flycatcher lives on insects taken on the wing, but often drops to the ground to take an earthworm or beetle, and seldom returns to the same perch like its relation the Spotted Flycatcher.

It has a lively little song on two up-and-down notes 'zee-it, zee-it, zee-it', with occasional trills.

The nest is built by the female of bark, moss, leaves, grass and lichen. There is a single clutch of usually five to eight eggs.

Pied Flycatchers are summer visitors, arriving from Africa about the end of April and returning in August and September.

Male Pied Flycatcher

Female Pied Flycatcher

Pied Wagtail ▲
Family Pipits and Wagtails

Pied Wagtails are the commonest of our three wagtails. They are often found near water, but seem equally at home on garden lawns or farms well away from water. Unfortunately, modern efficient farming methods are depriving these elegant little birds of many of the winged insects on which they feed.

Pied Wagtails often appear to be in perpetual motion and it is a delight to watch them. They seem to act on the impulse of the moment in their search for food – now running, standing, tail-wagging and then taking sudden vertical leaps in the air like a ballet dancer. Their flight is deeply undulating and they make a high-pitched 'tschizzik' flight call.

They nest in holes in walls, among creepers and in greenhouses where they also roost in winter. Pied Wagtails also have mass winter roosts in reed beds and in some city and town centres, where they find warmth, shelter and protection from predators.

The hen builds the nest of moss, dead leaves and twigs lined with hair and there are usually five or six eggs. Pied Wagtails are present all the year.

Redpoll ▶
Family Finches

Only twelve and a half centimetres long, this is one of our smaller finches. The Redpoll is a species which has benefited from the expansion of conifer plantations. There is a slight resemblance between Redpolls and Linnets but Linnets are larger. Redpolls are streaky grey-brown birds with crimson foreheads and black chins; the males have a pink flush on the breast. In winter they are often seen, in bounding flight, with Siskins and Goldfinches.

Their call is unmistakable, being a rapid 'chuch, uch, uch'. Redpolls live mainly on seeds, particularly of conifer, alder and birch; they also eat insects.

Redpolls, like Linnets, tend to nest in colonies and sometimes there are several nests in one bush. The nest is built by the hen of twigs and grass stalks and lined with down, hair or feathers. The use of grass gives the nest an untidy appearance. There are usually four to five eggs. Redpolls are present in the British Isles all the year. There are also winter visitors from the Continent and from Greenland.

Female Redstart

Redstart
Family Thrushes

The handsome little Redstarts are thirteen and a half centimetres long and easily spotted by their rusty red tails and rumps, which are seen as a bright flash when the birds are flying. They frequently quiver their fiery tails. The male has an orange breast and flanks, bluish-grey upperparts and a white forehead. The upperparts of the female are a light greyish-brown and the underparts orange-buff.

They have a Robin-like song, and in behaviour too Redstarts resemble the Robin, except that they are not so often seen on the ground, but flit about among the branches of trees and hover in the air to catch insects. The food taken is mainly insects and spiders.

Redstarts nest mainly in holes in trees, stumps and walls, sometimes close to the ground. The nest is built of grasses, pieces of bark, moss and roots and lined with hair and feathers. There are normally six eggs. Redstarts are summer visitors mainly to the north and west of Britain. They arrive in April and leave for their winter quarters in Africa during August.

Male Redstart

Redwing
Family Thrushes

This is our smallest thrush, only just over twenty centimetres long and mainly a winter visitor from Scandinavia, but there have been a few breeding records from northern Scotland and one from northern England.

It is very similar to the Song Thrush, but can be identified by the creamy eye-stripe and chestnut flanks. It is a winter visitor to woodlands and open fields, and comes into gardens in hard weather for berries.

We don't often hear the Redwing's song but just its thin feeble call 'see-ip' when it is flying over the coast at night during migration. Redwings eat worms, snails and slugs, insects and berries.

The nests in Scotland are usually in trees, bushes, stumps or on banks and are built from grass, twigs and earth lined with grass. There are five to six eggs. The Redwings arrive here mostly at the end of September and leave during April and early May.

Redwing

Robin
Family Thrushes

Our national bird and every gardener's favourite. Who can resist those large, dark, trusting eyes, the slender, delicate bill, the beacon-like breast and jaunty manner? Once a woodland bird, over the centuries the Robin has taken kindly to suburban gardens where it has become an enthusiastic regular at bird-tables. There is nothing it wouldn't do for a mealworm, but cheese and currants are highly acceptable.

The sexes are alike, but the young often confuse people by their plumage of speckled brown and buff with no red breast. The Robin obliges by singing almost throughout the year and how welcome that silvery thread of sound can be on a cold and dreary winter day.

Their natural food consists of insects, spiders, worms, also some seed, fruit and berries.

The nest might be almost anywhere. A hedge-bank, an ivy-covered wall, or it might be an old tin can, a bucket, or a kettle. It will be built of leaves and moss and lined with hair. There are five or six eggs and two, sometimes three broods.

Robins are present all the year, but there are winter movements south, some birds crossing to the Continent. Other Continental birds fly over to winter in England.

Siskin
Family Finches

One of our smaller finches, the male is yellowish-green with a black crown and chin, the underparts paler. The rump is yellow, and there are two yellow bars on the wing and yellow on the tail. In winter they flock, often with Redpolls. The Siskin sings almost continuous twittering notes.

These little birds are closely associated with conifers and the spread of forestry as they eat the seeds of conifers, alders and birches. This is helping them to increase their breeding range. An interesting development has been their discovery of peanuts hung up in net bags at bird-tables in winter. For some reason they come to red bags rather than to those of any other colour.

The nest is high up in conifers. The hen is the builder, using twigs, moss and grass lined with roots, down and hair. There are three to five eggs.

Siskins are mainly visitors to England and Wales, though some are present all the year in Scotland and Ireland and in some newly afforested areas of England and Wales.

Male Siskin

Female Siskin

51

Song Thrush (Female left, Male right)

Song Thrush ▲
Family Thrushes

The Song Thrush is smaller than the Mistle Thrush and browner in colour. The breast, a bright buff, has smaller spots, but its method of feeding is very like its larger relative. When seen standing in the open it is not quite so erect. It is one of our best loved songsters, loud and musical, with each phrase repeated twice and sometimes even five times. It frequently sings well into the dusk and is then mistaken for a Nightingale.

Song Thrushes feed on worms, snails and slugs, also on insects and they take fruit and berries. In mid-summer they often select a stone or small rock in a garden and use it as an anvil against which they beat the snail to crack the shell. They nest in hedges, bushes and trees, sometimes on banks or in sheds. The nest is built by the hen, and is made of grasses, roots, moss, leaves and earth. She lines it with mud which sets quite hard. There are four to five eggs.

Song Thrushes are present all the year. Some of our birds move south in winter and we also have winter visitors from the Continent.

Sparrowhawk
Family Kites, Buzzards, Hawks, Eagles, Harriers

The Sparrowhawk became very rare about 1959-60, mainly through the use of poisonous agricultural chemicals and also because of the destruction of hedges, and persecution by gamekeepers. There was a partial recovery in the 1970s and now the numbers seem to be recovering well.

They are dashing birds of prey, hunting along hedges and the edges of woods and taking their prey by surprise. Their main call is 'kek, kek, kek'.

The male has slate grey upperparts and underparts thickly barred with red-brown. The wings are round, not pointed like a falcon's, and the tail is long. Females are brown above and have whitish underparts barred with dark brown.

Sparrowhawks take small birds and mammals, and insects.

They generally nest in conifers in mixed woods and the nest is built mainly by the hen, of twigs, with leaves and bits of dead wood as a lining. There are four to five eggs. Sparrowhawks are present all the year in the British Isles.

Spotted Flycatcher
Family Flycatchers

This little bird can be identified mainly by its behaviour. It perches in a very upright pose and darts off to catch a flying insect, often returning to its original post. Otherwise, it is just a plain, light-brown, nondescript little bird, thirteen and a half centimetres long with a spotted crown and a white breast lightly streaked with brown.

Its call is a faint 'tzee' or 'tzee-tuc-tuc' something like that of a Redstart and its song is very weak. Spotted Flycatchers eat insects, most of which they catch on the wing. They nest on a support, such as a branch against a wall or tree trunk. The nest is built by both sexes of moss, wool and hair held together by cobwebs. There are four to five eggs.

The Spotted Flycatcher is a summer visitor to the British Isles from Africa, arriving usually during May and leaving from July to mid-September.

Male Sparrowhawk

Female Sparrowhawk

Starling
Family Starlings

At first sight a blackish bird, but on closer inspection in its summer plumage the feathers are glossed with green and purple. In winter the plumage is very speckled and the juveniles are mouse brown. The Starling has quite a long beak and a short tail. It can imitate other birds and mechanical sounds and has an extraordinary song consisting of whistles, chuckles, rattles and clicks. The flight is fast and direct with frequent glides. On the ground they walk with a jerky waddle.

Starlings eat both animal and vegetable food and cause damage to fruit crops. Their large communal roosts in trees and on city buildings also make them a nuisance. They nest almost everywhere in holes including nest boxes. The nest is started by the male before he finds a mate and then finished by the female. It is built of straw and lined with feathers. There are five to seven eggs.

Starlings are present all the year in the British Isles and our birds are joined in winter by large numbers of birds from the Continent.

Swallow
Family Swallows

Swallows can be identified by their continuous dark blue upperparts (which look black at a distance) and long tail streamers. They also have chestnut throats and foreheads and white underparts. They usually begin to arrive from their winter quarters in South Africa from early April. By the end of the month they are here in force: summer has begun. Their song is a continuous warbling and twittering, with a short sharp call 'tswit'.

Swallows eat insects which they catch in flight with agile grace.

They build their nests on rafters in sheds and other buildings and often return year after year to the same nest. It is built by both sexes from mud and straw like those of the House Martin, but the Swallow's nest is more saucer-shaped. There are four to five eggs.

Swallows are summer visitors to the British Isles; they start to leave during July.

Swift
Family Swifts

This is one of the three species which nest on buildings and hunt food on the wing, but Swifts are not related to Swallows and Martins, and don't resemble them much, except in behaviour. They are sooty black birds with whitish chins and short forked tails. The long narrow sickle-shaped wings beat very rapidly as the birds dash through the air with gaping bills, seeking the insects on which they live. It has been estimated that they can fly at 96 kph.

The commonest sound they make is a high-pitched scream, mostly in flight, but they will also call from the nest. This accounts for one of their country names: Devil Birds. Swifts are especially interesting because of their almost continuous life on the wing; in fact, from observations, it is thought that they may even sleep in the air too. As they are so seldom used, their legs are very weak and the four toes all point forward.

They nest in crevices under eaves, in holes in thatch, sometimes in old House Martins' nests. The nest is composed of vegetable fragments which the birds pick up in flight and stick together with saliva. There are two or three eggs.

The Swift is a summer visitor to the British Isles from South Africa, arriving in May and leaving in August.

Tawny Owl
Family Owls

This is our most common owl and can be found not only in woods, but also in suburban parks and gardens and even in town centres. The plumage is composed of warm colours, the upperparts speckled brown or greyish, the underparts buffish with large dark streaks. The voice is the best identification feature. Its call is 'ke-wick' and its song a long mellow hooting, one long clear note followed by three short notes, and ending with a long, quavering hoot.

It is seldom seen in a wood by day. If it should show itself a host of small birds will mob it.

These owls eat small mammals, birds, insects and worms and bring up the fur, feathers and bones in cigar-shaped pellets which may be found under the places where they roost during the day. They nest in holes in trees, in the old nests of crows or in special nest boxes. There is no nest material. There are two to four white eggs.

Tawny owls do not occur in Ireland, but are present all the year in Great Britain.

Tawny Owl

Tree Sparrow
Family Sparrows

The Tree Sparrow is often found where there are old trees and usually nests in holes and sometimes in nest boxes. A likely place might be a park where there is old timber, an overgrown orchard, the bank of a river or a big garden. The nest is built of straw and lined with feathers.

It is a slightly smaller version of the House Sparrow but differs in that the sexes are alike. The hen and the cock both have chestnut crowns and smart black bibs. They also differ from their more common relation in having a distinct black patch on each cheek. Tree Sparrows eat seeds and insects: outside the breeding season they feed on fields of stubble.

The Tree Sparrow makes shriller chirpings than the House Sparrow.

There are five or six eggs and two or three broods. Tree Sparrows are present all the year in the British Isles.

Treecreeper
Family Treecreepers

This little bird can climb trees like a mouse. It is twelve and a half centimetres long, has upperparts brown streaked with buff and underparts white. There is a whitish eye-stripe and the beak is thin, rather long and curved downwards. Unlike the Nuthatch, it only climbs upwards on trees or along branches, often in spiralling movement, then flies off to another tree where it again starts at the base. Its call is one shrill note rather slowly repeated. There is a song, but it is not very distinctive.

Treecreepers eat small insects which they find by probing with their bills in the bark.

The nest is built by both sexes behind loose pieces of bark and is made of twigs, moss, roots and grass. There are six eggs.

Treecreepers are present all the year in the British Isles.

Waxwing
Family Waxwings ▲

Waxwings are winter visitors from Finland and Russia, variable numbers appearing here every winter, but usually in Eastern Britain. When there is a big invasion it is said to be a 'Waxwing Winter'. They come in little flocks and may be seen in large gardens, woodland and open country, wherever there are berries to be had. Some people think they are seeing exotic birds from an aviary. They can be identified by the pinky-chestnut crest and yellow-tipped tail. The upperparts are pinkish-brown and the underparts pinkish. The wings are dark with white and yellow markings. The throat is black and the rump grey. The bird's name comes from the wax-like red tips to the secondary wing-feathers – that is, the feathers half-way up the wing when it is folded – but these are not very conspicuous. When moving about in flocks they call constantly to each other with a soft trilling sound.

Waxwings visit us from October to March.

Willow Warbler
Family Warblers

This little warbler (eleven centimetres long) is so similar to the Chiffchaff that if it weren't for their songs they would be hard indeed to tell apart. The Willow Warbler is greenish above, yellowish below and has a pale eye-stripe. Like other warblers, it is constantly on the move, singing while it hunts among the leaves and twigs for insects.

Its call is like that of the Chiffchaff, 'hooeet', but its song is totally different – a lovely liquid descending phrase of wistful notes, once heard not to be forgotten.

Willow Warblers eat insects, spiders and sometimes small worms. They eat some berries in autumn.

They nest among grass in hedge-bottoms and other similar places on the ground. The hen builds the domed nest of moss, stalks and grasses; the lining is of feathers. There are six to seven eggs.

Willow Warblers are summer visitors to the British Isles from Africa. They arrive towards the end of March and leave from mid-July. ▼

Woodcock ▲
Family Sandpipers, Godwits, Curlews and Snipe

The Woodcock is the only wader to have taken to woodland. Its plumage of russet with bars on the head and underparts serves as a marvellous camouflage. In fact it is more likely to see you, as its eyes are set high and to the back of the head, so that it has all-round vision. The best chance of seeing one is at dusk or dawn when the male makes a regular display flight round its territory – this is called 'roding'. When flushed during the day it weaves away, dodging among the tree trunks. The Woodcock eats worms, insects and some seeds.

Woodcocks nest on the ground among bracken or brambles. The nest is a hollow lined with dead leaves. There are four eggs. If the young are in danger the female may lift them to safety, clutching them between her thighs.

Woodcocks are present all the year in Britain. Some migrate south of their breeding range. Others arrive from Northern Europe in November to spend the winter here.

As game birds, they are only protected during the 'close season'. This is from February to the end of August, although for Woodcock in England and Wales there is an extension to 30th September.

Woodpigeon ▶
Family Pigeons and Doves

A large, gentle-looking bird, but regarded as an agricultural pest. In a hard winter it can soon strip a market garden and all the year round it ravages farm crops. They are stout birds, blue-grey, with a broad white wing stripe and white patches on the sides of the neck, which is glossed with purple and green.

The song has a strong beat – '*coo* coo coo-coo, *coo*', the last note abrupt. Most of their food is vegetable, although they also take worms, slugs, snails and insects.

Woodpigeons nest in woodland trees and in hedges. They have also adapted successfully to town parks and gardens. The nest is an openwork platform of small twigs. There are two white eggs. The hen incubates by night and the cock by day. The young are fed on 'pigeon's milk' (*see* Collared Dove).

The Woodpigeon is present all the year in Britain.

Wood Warbler ▲
Family Warblers

The Wood Warbler is larger than the
Chiffchaff and Willow Warbler and brighter,
having yellow-green upperparts and yellow
underparts. It also has a yellow eye-stripe. The
song, heard mostly in woodland, is 'whit, whit,
whit' followed by a shivering trill. It also has a
plaintive sustained piping note which reminds
people of the Nightingale. Wood Warblers eat
mostly insects.

They nest mainly in woodland, building a
domed nest on the ground of dead leaves and lined
with fine grass stems. There are six to seven eggs.

Wood Warblers are summer visitors from
Africa, arriving here generally during the third
week of April and beginning to leave from the
end of July. They rarely occur in Ireland.

Wren
Family Wrens

◀   These perky little birds can hardly be missed
with their tiny, cocked tails and mouse-like
behaviour. The warm brown plumage is closely
barred and there is a pale eye-stripe.

The call is 'tic, tic, tic', harsher than the similar
call of the Robin, and the trilling song is

58

exceptionally loud for the bird's size. Wrens eat insects, spiders and seeds.

They nest in hedges and on banks, in holes and nest boxes. The cock builds several nests called 'cocks' nests' of moss and grass. The hen chooses the one she likes best and lines it with feathers. It is domed, with a side entrance. There are five to six eggs.

Wrens cannot stand hard winters and often bundle together to keep warm. They do not come to bird-tables. However, scraps of cheese sprinkled on the ground among twigs and dried leaves will be found and eaten.

Wrens are present all the year in the British Isles.

Wryneck
Family Woodpeckers

This rather mysterious bird does not look much like a woodpecker, although it has woodpecker feet: two toes in front, two behind. It is small, only sixteen centimetres long, the upperparts being grey-brown and very mottled and streaked. The underparts are paler and barred with brown and the longish tail is rounded at the end and barred grey and brown. It has the habit of perching along a branch, not across it, and climbs trees like a woodpecker. The name comes from its habit of twisting its head right round like a snake. The call of the Wryneck is a shrill 'quee-quee-quee-quee'.

It is becoming very rare as a breeding bird in Britain.

Wrynecks feed on insects, woodlice and spiders. They nest in holes in trees, nest boxes, in banks, thatch or walls. There is no nest material. There are seven to ten eggs.

Wrynecks used to be regular summer visitors to England and Wales. They arrived from Africa from the end of March and left again from the end of July. There has been a serious reduction in the Wryneck population from the late 1940s – there were no breeding records in England in 1974, and only a few from Scotland. These birds are now more commonly observed as migrants travelling between Scandinavia and their winter quarters in Southern Asia and tropical Africa.

Birds of
Heath and
Farmland

Barn Owl
Family Barn Owls

These attractive owls with their heart-shaped faces and feathered legs are farmers' friends because they eat rats and mice. A pair of Barn Owls feeding young have been known to bring a mouse to their nest every fifteen minutes. Sadly, there are fewer old barns in the tidy, efficient countryside of today and the owls' numbers are declining.

In colour they are orange-buff above, faintly speckled, and white below. The face is white and the eyes black. They fly mostly at dusk, hunting over the ground in a search for prey. Their voice is like a long, wild shriek – also hissing and snoring when hunting.

They eat (as well as rats and mice) voles, shrews and small birds. The indigestible parts are brought up as pellets (*see* Tawny Owl).

The nest is usually in farm buildings, church towers, ruins, etc. There are four to six eggs.

Barn Owls are present all the year in the British Isles and are found almost all over the world.

Carrion Crow
Family Crows

This bird is unpopular with game-keepers because it is a great egg thief. It will also attack sickly small animals and birds. Like other members of the crow family, it is quick to learn and on the coast has learnt to break open mussels by dropping them from a height.

Crows can be distinguished from Rooks by the greenish gloss on their black plumage, not purple. Note too that the base of the thick black bill is fully feathered, unlike the Rook's bare grey patch. In addition, the Crow lacks the 'baggy trousers' of the Rook.

Carrion Crows have expanded to many towns and cities. The bird has even a call which sounds quite like a motor horn, although the usual one is a deep, harsh 'Kraah'.

They are not seen in such big colonies as Rooks, but are often in family parties especially in autumn and winter. At other times they may be solitary or in a pair.

They will eat almost anything.

The bulky nest of twigs is usually in the fork of a high tree or on a cliff ledge. There are three to five eggs.

Carrion Crows are present all the year in Britain.

Cirl Bunting
Family Buntings

One of our lesser-known buntings, found mainly in south-west England. They resemble Yellowhammers at first sight, but the females have more yellow underneath than the female Yellowhammer and the male has yellow underparts with a greenish breastband, a black throat and black and yellow on the face.

The song is a short jingle on one note, from a song post such as a tall tree or telegraph wires.

Cirl Buntings eat corn, grass and weed seeds, berries and insects. They sometimes feed in flocks with other seed-eaters. The nest, built by the hen, is in hedges, gorse-bushes and brambles. It is made of grass, roots and moss, lined with fine grasses and horsehair.

Cirl Buntings are resident in south-west England but wander elsewhere in the United Kingdom during the winter.

Cirl Bunting (Male left, Female right)   *courtship feeding*

They have a whirring flight and frequently glide on down-turned wings.

Partridges feed on weeds and grain, insects, earthworms and slugs. They nest at the bottom of hedges, on waste ground with bushes and in fields of corn. There are usually twelve to eighteen eggs, laid in a scrape made by the hen. The chicks are able to leave the nest almost at once.

They are present all the year in the British Isles.

Male Common Partridge

Common Partridge
Family Partridges and Pheasants

This is a typical bird of farmland, occurring principally in corn-growing districts but also on grassland. It is usually now called the Grey Partridge. It is a stout bird with a rust-coloured head and a grey neck and breast. The male has a conspicuous chestnut mark, shaped like a horseshoe, on the lower breast, while the flanks of the female are broadly barred.

Female Common Partridge

beak. The song is the best identification feature, being a short rapid jingle which sounds rather like the rattling of a bunch of keys.

Corn Buntings mainly eat vegetable matter – weed and grass seeds, leaves, buds, berries – but also insects. The hen builds the untidy nest in long grass and weeds, or sometimes in a bush above the ground. There are three to five eggs.

Corn Buntings are present all the year in the British Isles, although many breeding birds leave us in the autumn. They are mostly found on the eastern side of England and Scotland.

Corn Bunting
Family Buntings

This is our largest bunting and another typical bird of farmland. It is usually seen singing from the top of a hedge or from a telegraph wire at the side of the road. It is a portly bird, streaked brown above and below and has a short thick

Corncrake
Family Crakes and Coots

This species is now only common in Ireland and very rare in other parts of the British Isles. It is a shy, skulking bird of rough grassland and hardly ever seen; its presence can usually only be known by its song, a rough 'crek, crek'. When seen it is a chicken-like bird, buff in colour marked blackish above with a grey head and breast. In flight, the legs are trailed behind the body. Corncrakes have probably declined in numbers because of modern haymaking methods.

Corncrakes mainly eat insects. They nest in grass and thick vegetation; the nest is usually just a hollow in the ground and made by the hen. There are normally eight to twelve eggs.

Corncrakes are summer visitors from southern Africa, arriving here in April and leaving from the end of July.

Corncrake

Dartford Warbler ▲
Family Warblers

This is our only wintering warbler and now under serious threat because of the destruction in Britain of gorsy heathland. It is very vulnerable to hard winters and there are probably only a few pairs left in southern England, in spite of the fact that a special reserve has been set up to protect them.

The males have bushy, dark grey heads and dark brown upperparts; the underparts are wine-red. The tail is long, narrowing at the end and is often held cocked. This is a skulking bird, very hard to see, except during the breeding season when the male perches on the tops of gorse bushes.

They have a short song, a warble like that of a Whitethroat, and a harsh 'tchirr' alarm note.

Dartford Warblers eat nothing but insects.

The nest is usually in long heather or gorse. There are three to four eggs.

Dartford Warblers are present all the year although now very rare.

Fieldfare ▶
Family Warblers, Flycatchers, Thrushes, etc.

These Scandinavian thrushes come to us for the winter and breed, in very small numbers, in Scotland and a few secret places in England. They are a little smaller than Mistle Thrushes and more brightly coloured, with grey heads and rumps, chestnut backs and blackish tails.

Their call is a harsh 'tchak-tchak-tchak', often heard in autumn from the night sky as the migrants arrive over the coast.

They eat slugs, worms, insects, spiders and berries, fallen apples, grain and seed.

The Fieldfare, where it has nested in Britain, has chosen a variety of locations: farmland, scrub, hill slopes, forestry plantations, the banks of streams or high up in trees. The nest is similar to that of the Blackbird. There are five or six eggs.

As winter visitors, Fieldfares start to arrive here during the last week of September and leave from April onwards.

Great Grey Shrike
Family Shrikes ▲

This is the largest of the shrikes, a rare winter visitor to the eastern side of Great Britain from northern Europe. Their behaviour helps to identify them because they are usually seen perched on the tops of trees or bushes watching for prey which they fly down to the ground to catch. They are striking-looking birds with grey foreheads, crowns and backs, black beaks, a long black patch through the eye and black wings and tails. The underparts are white and there are white edges to the flight feathers of the wings. There is also a white tip to the tail as well as a narrow white eye-stripe over their black patch.

The alarm call is a harsh 'shek, shek'.

They eat small birds, small mammals, insects, frogs, lizards and slow-worms.

Great Grey Shrikes visit from the beginning of October onwards, even as late as May.

Grasshopper Warbler
Family Warblers

A secretive, skulking bird, it would often go undetected but for its mechanical song, a peculiar 'reeling' sound. This high pitched trill can last for one or two minutes, sounding near then far away as the bird moves its head from side to side as it sings. It quite frequently sings at night, as well as in the day.

Most of its time is spent low down in thick undergrowth, in places where there is plenty of cover such as heathland, downland and particularly marshy areas. ◄

It is almost mouse-like as it scuttles about searching for insects, spiders and the like and only when it sings from an exposed perch can one see it is not a very colourful bird, being olive brown with a dark streaked back and buffish underparts. However, the rounded tail is a distinctive feature and when flushed from the undergrowth, this and the oval shaped wings should aid identification.

The nest, built entirely of dead grass with a finer grass lining is well hidden near the ground. The five to six eggs are pinkish, sometimes purplish-grey and marked with fine red-brown speckles. A summer visitor, it arrives in late April, leaving again in August and September.

It is widely distributed throughout Britain and Ireland in suitable habitats.

Hobby with young

Hobby
Family Falcons

This is one of our smaller birds of prey. It is a dashing flyer with scythe-shaped wings and can be mistaken for a large swift. The difference is that as a bird of prey it is usually accompanied by a party of small birds, mobbing it.

At close range, the Hobby can be identified by its chestnut thighs and by the chestnut colour beneath the tail.

Hobbies sometimes take small birds on the wing, also insects and small mammals, and on warm summer evenings they often hawk for cockchafers or even bats.

They do not build a nest but use the unoccupied nests of other birds, mainly the Carrion Crow. They favour Scots Pines, heaths and downs, but may also be seen in mixed farmland.

The number of eggs is normally three.

Hobbies are summer visitors to Britain, usually to southern England, arriving towards the end of April. Their winter quarters are in Africa.

Hooded Crow ▶
Family Crows

This is the crow which takes the place of the Carrion Crow in the north of Britain and Ireland. It can be easily identified because it looks like a Carrion Crow wearing a grey sleeveless pullover.

The 'Hoodie' is in fact a different form of the Carrion Crow and they sometimes inter-breed. Its voice is like that of its close relative, a harsh croak 'kraa, kraa, kraa'.

Hooded Crows eat carrion, birds, small mammals, birds' eggs, frogs, insects and worms and some vegetable food. These birds are particularly unpopular with gamekeepers on grouse moors as they eat the chicks.

They nest mainly in trees and both sexes build. The nest is of sticks, heather, moss and earth, lined with wool and hair. There are four to six eggs.

Hooded Crows are present all the year in Scotland and Ireland and are autumn and winter visitors to England and Wales.

Lapwing
Family Plovers

The Lapwing is a wader, and an exceptionally handsome bird. Not all waders are now associated with water and the Lapwing is a typical bird of farmland. It is also called Green Plover and, from its call, Peewit. It forms into flocks in winter and is then more often seen in wet places. Recognition is easy because of the elegant thin crest, black breast above white underparts and metallic green back. It has broad wings and a slow, flapping flight. In spring it performs a striking aerobatic display over the breeding grounds.

Lapwings eat mainly insects, slugs, snails and worms but also vegetable matter, seeds and grass.

They nest on the ground, the nest is just a hollow lined with grass. There are usually four eggs. The chicks leave the nest as soon as their down is dry. Lapwings are present all the year in the British Isles, but large numbers come from the Continent in the autumn.

Linnet
Family Finches

In the breeding season the cock Linnet has a crimson forehead and breast. The back is chestnut, the head grey and the underparts are buff, streaked with blackish-brown. The forked tail has white edgings.

Linnets have a bounding flight and in winter form flocks with other finches over fields of stubble or rough country near the coast.

The Linnet is a seed-eater, but it also takes insects.

The typical nest site is close to the ground in a bush but it will also nest in thickets of bramble and in thorn bushes, in hedges and in gardens. The hen builds the nest of stalks, grass, moss and twigs and lines it with hair, wool or feathers. Sometimes several birds will nest together.

The eggs number from four to six.

Linnets are present all the year in the British Isles, but some young birds move south in the autumn, many crossing the Channel.

Male Linnet

Female Linnet

Lesser Whitethroat ▲
Family Warblers

A slightly smaller and greyer looking version of the Whitethroat, it lacks the warm brown of the wings found in the other bird while the darker grey area on the face gives it a masked appearance.

The song is also quite different, being a succession of loud notes not unlike a Yellowhammer. This 'rattle' which is the best way to describe it, is often, though not always, preceded by a soft low musical warble, but this can only be heard at very close range. Tall thick hedgerows and large overgrown gardens are the haunt of this bird. It builds a small round nest of stalks and roots, often lined with horsehair. The four to six eggs are creamy white, sparsely blotched with dark markings.

A summer visitor, it arrives in April returning to Africa in August or September. During its stay it feeds mainly on insects but in the autumn some fruits and berries are eaten.

Generally distributed throughout England, it becomes rarer northwards, being entirely absent from Scotland. It is also scarce in Wales and there are none nesting in Ireland.

Little Owl
Family Owls

◄ This is our smallest owl and it was introduced into England and Wales from the Continent last century. It is a compact little bird with a large head and staring yellow eyes; the upperparts are grey-brown spotted with white and the underparts white streaked brown. When alarmed, it bobs up and down in a comical way. It is a bird of the open countryside and may be seen perching on posts, branches, and walls in daylight. The commonest call is a cat-like 'kiew, kiew'.

The food of the Little Owl is mainly animal – rodents, small birds, lizards and frogs, insects, slugs, snails and worms.

It nests in tree holes and sometimes in old buildings or cliffs. There are three to five white eggs.

It is present all the year in England and Wales.

Meadow Pipit ▲
Family Pipits and Wagtails

This species is found in many different kinds of rough open country including mountain moorland. It is not easy to identify, being just a little brown bird, streaked all over with blackish-brown and with white outer tail-feathers. The best clue is the song-flight – the bird flies up from the ground to about thirty metres, singing a thin, feeble song, then glides down again still singing.

Meadow Pipits eat mainly insects, worms, spiders and sometimes seeds.

They nest in hollows on the ground, in clumps of grass, rushes or heather. The nest is built of grass, lined with fine grass and horsehair. There are three or four eggs. The nest is often used by Cuckoos for their eggs.

Meadow Pipits are present all the year in the British Isles although many winter in south-west Europe.

Nightjar ▶
Family Nightjars

A mysterious bird of the night. In the daytime it is almost invisible thanks to its markings, the colour of dead leaves, as it lies motionless on the ground.

At dusk the Nightjar leaves its hiding place and in silent flight on long hawk-like wings chases flying insects, trapping them in its gaping bill. It is then that its strange churring sound is heard, as it perches, usually along, not across, the branch of a tree. It also has a flight-call – a soft 'coo-ic' and makes a whip-crack sound by clapping its wings together.

Nightjars nest on heaths, on hillsides among bracken and in woodland clearings. The eggs are laid in a scrape on the ground. There are two eggs; the hen sits during the day and the cock by night.

Nightjars are summer visitors to the British Isles from Africa.

Pheasant
Family Partridges and Pheasants

This is a game-bird which was originally brought here from Asia Minor and followed by other races from China, Japan and Mongolia. These different races have interbred and what we have now is a hybrid.

The male is exotically coloured with a long tail,

Male Pheasant

70

a metallic dark green head, red wattles round the eye and small ear-like tufts on the crown. There is usually a white neck ring. The back is a mottled brown and the tail has black bars on brown. The female is plain brown.

The cock crows with a loud 'Korr-Kok'.

Pheasants eat mainly vegetable food – leaves, weed seeds, grain, roots, nuts, peas, beans, potatoes and also insects, worms, slugs and snails.

They nest in copses, under hedges and on waste ground. The nest is a hollow scraped by the hen, usually under vegetation and there are eight to fifteen eggs.

Pheasants are present all the year in the British Isles.

Female Pheasant

Red-backed Shrike
Family Shrikes

Called 'butcher-bird' because they hang their prey, mainly beetles and bees, on thorn bushes in 'larders'. These are rare birds now and restricted to south-east England, although they used to nest throughout England and Wales. They are colourful birds, the male with a chestnut back, blue-grey crown and rump, a black tail with white patches, a black patch through the eye and a hooked black beak. The female is brown with a barred breast. The call is a harsh 'chack'.

Red-backed Shrikes eat insects, small birds, rodents, lizards and frogs.

They nest in bramble clumps, bushes and hedges, the nest being built mainly by the male of moss and grass, lined with roots and hair. There are four to six eggs.

Red-backed Shrikes are rare summer visitors to south-east England, wintering in Africa.

Female Red-backed Shrike 71   *Male Red-backed Shrike*

Red-legged Partridge
Family Partridges and Pheasants ▲

This game-bird was introduced into Great Britain about two hundred years ago. It is larger than the Common or Grey Partridge. The Red-legged has black and white eye-stripes, a grey crown, grey sides boldly barred with chestnut and black, and red beak and legs. It stands higher and more erect than the Common Partridge.

The voice is a challenging 'chucka, chucka'.

They are birds of farmland, sandy heaths, coastal shingle and chalk downs and eat mainly vegetable food.

They nest under hedges, in fields of crops and on waste places. The nest is a scrape in the ground lined with dead leaves and grass. There are ten to sixteen eggs.

Red-legged Partridges are present all the year in England and Wales.

Rook ▼
Family Crows

Rooks differ from Crows in having a purplish gloss on their black plumage and there is a patch of greyish white skin round the base of the bill. Another difference is that the Rook has thick thigh feathers like baggy trousers. They walk sedately, but have a rather heavy flight.

Rooks live in colonies in farmland usually near human settlements. The Rookeries vary in size and the birds use the same nests year after year. They are near the tops of tall trees and built by both sexes of sticks. The lining is of dry grass, leaves, roots and moss. There are three to six eggs.

Rooks are present all the year in the British Isles.

Short-eared Owl
Family Owls

This is a large daytime owl, hunting by day and at dusk over open country. It is light brown in colour, marked with buff and dark brown. The wings are rounded. When hunting it quarters the ground in slow, flapping, flight. The ear-tufts are just small tufts of feathers. It is generally silent but has a harsh flight-call. The song is low and booming and in its spring display flight the wings are often clapped under the body.

Short-eared Owls feed mainly on small mammals especially voles, also birds and insects.

They nest in a scraped-out hollow in the ground and there are usually four to eight eggs, but more when there is a plague of field voles, to provide plenty of food.

These owls are partial migrants, residents and also winter visitors to the British Isles. In winter several may be seen together in suitable places – when voles are plentiful.

Skylark
Family Larks

Famous for its musical song-flight and a favourite bird of poets. The upperparts are brown, streaked with black, the underparts are paler; there is a small crest and white feathers in the tail.

The famous song is a high-pitched, loud, clear warbling uttered in flight when ascending, the bird continues singing while hovering and also when descending. Its call is a trilled 'chirrup'. The song is sometimes heard from the ground or from a song post.

Skylarks eat weed seeds, corn and leaves, also worms and insects. The nest is a cup on the ground, of grass lined with fine grass and sometimes hair. There are three to four eggs.

Skylarks are present all the year in the British Isles. Large numbers come here from Central Europe in winter. ▼

Short-eared Owl

Short-eared Owl at nest

Stock Dove
Family Pigeons and Doves

Stock Doves are sometimes mistaken for Woodpigeons. They are smaller, and with no white on the wings or neck. The colour is dark blue-grey with a green gloss on the neck and there are two small black bars on the wings that show clearly in flight. They have a double 'coo' note, much gruffer and shorter than the Woodpigeon.

Stock Doves eat similar food – grain, leaves, peas and beans.

They nest in holes in trees, rocks and buildings, sometimes in rabbit burrows. There are two eggs.

They are present all the year in the British Isles.

Male Stonechat

Female Stonechat

Stonechat
Family Warblers, Flycatchers, Thrushes, etc.

This is a plump little bird of heathland and gorsy commons. Stonechats are easy to see and identify because they perch on bushes or posts flirting their tails and attracting attention by their 'tack, tack' call. They are attractive birds, the male having a black head and throat with a white patch on each side of the neck, a chestnut breast, a white rump and a dark brown back and tail. The female is a duller version.

Stonechats eat insects chiefly, also spiders and worms.

They nest on the ground, under a bush or similar place and the nest is built of moss and grasses lined with stems and hair. There are five to six eggs.

Stonechats are present all the year in the British Isles. They are becoming rarer in eastern and central England.

74

Stone Curlew
Family Stone Curlews

A mysterious bird, it is particularly active at dusk when it may be heard calling with its plaintive 'coo-ee' note.

It is not easy to see, for its streaked sandy brown plumage renders it almost invisible against a background of stony soil, the sort of habitat it prefers.

Like a large plover with pale yellow legs and large yellow eyes, its appearance is unmistakable. It moves with great stealth and if disturbed, takes short pattering steps with its head lowered and neck withdrawn. When frightened it 'freezes' in a flattened position, head and neck extended, relying on its camouflage to protect it from discovery. In flight however, it reveals a conspicuous wing pattern of two bold whitish bars.

Its food comprises a variety of items from snails to slugs, worms and insects.

The nest is often quite a deep scrape invariably lined with small stones or rabbit droppings, usually on bare ground. The two rounded eggs are buff or stone coloured, irregularly spotted, streaked and blotched with dark brown.

A few may winter in southern England but it is mainly a summer visitor to Britain arriving in March or April and leaving around October time.

Numbers have decreased considerably in recent years, mainly due to loss of habitat. There are now probably less than five hundred pairs, most of which are to be found in the Brecklands of East Anglia and the downlands of Wiltshire.

Tree Pipit
Family Pipits

Like other pipits this bird has no distinctive plumage coloration, being generally brownish and streaked with dark markings. Confusion is most likely to occur between this bird and the Meadow Pipit, but the sleeker appearance and less streaking on the more buff coloured breast should aid identification. Also, the legs are distinctly flesh-coloured and if seen at really close range, the short hind claw may be detected.

Though the two species can occur together on migration, this bird is more frequently found in open woodland, heathland and parkland, or areas of grassland where there are scattered trees. In this type of habitat its characteristic song-flight will be seen. The bird flutters upwards from the top of a tree, and near the peak of its ascent, begins to sing, 'see-er, see-er, see-er' continuing as it parachutes down, generally returning to the same or a nearby perch.

The nest is usually a depression in the ground. The four to six eggs have a remarkable colour range from pale blue to greenish to pinkish brown or grey, being freckled all over or blotched or spotted. A summer visitor, it is common in parts of England and Wales, becoming scarcer northwards into Scotland. It does not breed in Ireland.

Turtle Dove
Family Pigeons and Doves

This is a summer visitor mainly to southern and eastern parts of England from Africa, and our only migrant dove. It is the smallest and slimmest of the family; the tail is long and blackish with a white tip which shows clearly in flight. Otherwise it is reddish-brown above with a pinkish throat and breast and a patch of black and white striped feathers on both sides of the neck.

Its song is a sleepy repeated purr, a drowsy summery sound: 'the voice of the turtle' heard in the Song of Solomon.

Turtle Doves are largely birds of open country. They eat some corn on stubble fields and leaves and weed seeds, especially of the one called fumitory.

They nest in bushes, tall hedges and orchards. The nest is a flat platform of twigs. There are two eggs.

They arrive towards the end of April and leave again from early August onwards.

Wheatear
Family Warblers, Flycatchers, Thrushes, etc.

This is a handsome, perky little bird which lives on the ground in open country. It arrives in early March from winter quarters in Africa. The male has blue-grey upperparts, a black patch on each side of the face under a white stripe, black wings and lower tail. A distinctive white rump and upper part of the tail show clearly in flight. The underparts are sandy-buff. The female has brown upperparts and buff underparts, dark brown where the male is black, but has the same white on rump and tail.

The call is a harsh 'chack-chack' and the song a squeaky little warble from a song-post or in flight.

Wheatears eat insects, centipedes and spiders.

They nest in holes in the ground sometimes in rabbit burrows, or in crevices in rocks, walls and similar places. There are six eggs.

Wheatears are summer visitors mainly to northern and western Britain from Africa. They are becoming rarer in the south of England. Greenland Wheatears are seen passing through in spring and autumn.

Female Wheatear

Male Wheatear

76

Whinchat
Family Warblers, Flycatchers, Thrushes, etc.

Whinchats begin to arrive in mid-April after wintering in Africa. They are found on all kinds of rough grassland on heaths, commons, hillsides, and sometimes even on railway embankments. It is the only small brown bird with a distinctive white eye-stripe, the female's is duller. Both sexes have white sides to base of tail. The face is dark and the cock has a pinkish breast.

They perch to sing on bushes or tall plants. The song is a short warble and the call-note consists of odd clicking noises. The flight is low and jerky from one point to another and they sometimes perch like Flycatchers, then flutter into the air to catch insects. Whinchats find most of their insect food on the ground.

The nest is also on the ground in rough vegetation. There are five to six eggs.

Whinchats are summer visitors to Great Britain from Africa. They are becoming rarer in central and south-east England.

Male Whinchat

Female Whinchat

Male Whitethroat

Female Whitethroat

Whitethroat
Family Warblers, Flycatchers, Thrushes, etc.

Whitethroats arrive in this country from Africa about the third week of April and leave again in the autumn. They are warblers and have all the restlessness of their relatives. The males in the breeding season have a grey cap, a white throat, rusty-brown wings and light pinkish underparts. Their alarm note is a rather cross 'tcharr' and the song is a short, brisk warble, scratchy in quality, sometimes given in an almost vertical dancing song-flight.

They eat insects and spiders but take some berries and fruit in autumn.

Whitethroats are birds of open country – heaths, commons, farmland, etc. They nest near the ground in bushes, hedge-bottoms and brambles, hence their country name of 'nettle-creeper'. The nest is built by the cock who makes several trial nests from which the hen can choose. It is a deep cup made of grasses lined with hair. There are four to five eggs.

Whitethroats are summer visitors to the British Isles.

Willow Tit
Family Titmice

This little bird has a relative which is so like it that it is almost impossible to tell them apart, except by their calls (*see* Marsh Tit). The best clue to the Willow Tit's identity is its low, gruff 'chay, chay'. Its crown is dull black rather than glossy, but that is not obvious. It also has a faint light wing-bar. Otherwise both species are alike – black chin, whitish cheeks and underparts, mantle, wings and tail brown. The Marsh Tit's distinctive call is 'pichu' but the Willow Tit has no call like it. ▼

Like all the tits, the Willow eats insects, also seeds and wild fruit.

Willow Tits are found in types of habitat different from that of the Marsh Tit, for Marsh Tits are mainly woodland birds, but Willow Tits like wetter places, especially in the breeding season.

They excavate their nesting holes in rotten wood and are not particularly interested in willow trees. Both sexes, but mainly the hen, do the work. The eggs are laid on a thin lining of hair or rabbit fur. There are six to nine eggs.

The Willow Tit is present all the year in England and Wales but not Ireland and it is rare in Scotland.

Woodlark ▲
Family Larks

These birds are smaller than Skylarks, they also have very short tails with no white feathers. The main difference is the song which is not as lively but sweeter than that of its relative. It is performed on the wing, the bird ascending in spirals and circling round singing. It also sings from a tree or bush and sometimes at night.

Woodlarks eat insects mainly, also spiders and seeds.

They nest on the ground in a deep depression and the nest is built by both sexes of grass stems and moss with a lining of fine grass. There are usually three to four eggs, which hatch in thirteen to fifteen days.

Woodlarks are present all the year in England but are confined now to the southern half of the country; they have suffered a decline in numbers in recent years.

Yellowhammer
Family Buntings

The Yellowhammer or Yellow Bunting as it is sometimes called has bright yellow head and underparts and chestnut brown upperparts streaked with black. The rump is plain chestnut. The female has much less yellow than the male but she also has the chestnut rump and both sexes have white outer tail feathers which show up in flight.

The song is a familiar sound of country lanes in summer and the words 'Little bit of bread and no cheese' (the 'cheese' higher pitched than the rest) describe it quite well.

They eat mainly vegetable matter – corn, weed seeds, wild fruits, etc., but also insects. After breeding they often flock with other seed-eaters over stubble fields.

Yellowhammers nest in hedges, by roadsides or in plantations of young trees, usually on or near the ground. The nest is made of grass stalks and moss lined with hair and fine grass.

They are present all the year in the British Isles.

Male Yellowhammer

Female Yellowhammer

Male Yellow Wagtail

Female Yellow Wagtail

Yellow Wagtail
Family Pipits and Wagtails

This wagtail is much more a bird of meadows, marshes and farmland than our other wagtails. Its tail is slightly shorter than that of the Pied and Grey Wagtails – sixteen centimetres long against their seventeen and a half centimetres. The male is a very yellow bird with bright yellow underparts and also a bright yellow eye-stripe and throat. The upperparts are greenish-brown. The female in summer is duller, brown above and paler below. The call is a shrill 'tsweep' and the song, a warble uttered from a perch or in bouncing flight.

Yellow Wagtails eat insects. They sometimes feed among herds of grazing animals, snatching at insects put up by the hoofs.

They breed among tall plants in water meadows, cornfields or in gardens. The nest is built by the hen on the ground, of grass stalks and roots, lined with cow or horsehair. There are usually six eggs.

Yellow Wagtails are summer visitors to the British Isles, arriving from Africa about the end of March and leaving from mid-August onwards.

Birds of Rivers Lakes Gravel-pits and Reservoirs

Black-headed Gull in summer

Black-headed Gull
Family Gulls and Terns

Most of our gulls are not true seabirds but rather birds of the coast, and the Black-headed Gull is rarely seen far from land. Its main identification features are its small size and in summer its chocolate brown (not black) hood. In winter, this disappears and is replaced by black marks like smudges in front of and behind the eye. The legs and beak are red, the wings pale grey with a white leading edge (the front edge) and black wing-tips. The underparts and neck are white.

The call consists of a series of various harsh notes.

These gulls are scavengers and eat almost anything, but mainly animal food.

They nest in colonies on islands in lakes, among sandhills and shingle by the sea or even far inland. The nest is untidy and made of any kind of vegetable matter, sometimes just a scrape. There are normally three eggs.

Black-headed Gulls are present all the year in the British Isles, and in winter they are joined by migrants from the Continent.

Black-headed Gull in winter

Black Tern
Family Terns

The only tern with all blackish breeding plumage, it is most frequently noticed in spring when flocks of these birds pass through on migration. On occasions one might see as many as a hundred or more as they fly back and forth over the water of some lake or reservoir, dipping to pick insects from the surface, rarely plunging in to feed. Its cry is a rather squeaky 'kit' note, but this is seldom uttered.

Called 'marsh terns' because they nest in colonies in the shallows of marshes and lagoons, the female lays two or three eggs in a nest of floating weed, though sometimes they will build on firm ground.

It bred regularly in east and south-east England at one time, but due to drainage and disturbance, ceased to do so by the middle of the last century.

In recent years however, small numbers have begun to nest again, particularly in the Ouse Washes where bird reserves are attracting back these and other lost breeding birds.

In the winter it loses its dark colouring and looks pale grey.

Fewer birds are usually noted on the return passage in the autumn, but there are often one or two still passing through in late October.

Black Tern

Black-throated Diver
Family Divers

Of our four species of divers only two breed here and this is one of them. In the breeding season they frequent large lochs of the Scottish Highlands and islands. In the winter they move to coastal waters, estuaries and sometimes lakes or reservoirs near the coast; occasionally to the large London reservoirs. They are superb swimmers but very clumsy on land.

In summer the Black-throated Diver has a most striking and complicated plumage pattern. The crown and back of the neck are grey; the rather long pointed bill, the throat and back are all black. The underparts are white and there are white stripes down each side of the neck and breast. A similar but bolder pattern of white stripes appears in two patches at each side of the back.

The call of this species is a hoarse 'kwuk-kwuk-kwuk' and like other divers it has a weird, wailing cry.

Black-throats eat animal food only – mostly fish.

The nest is merely a flattened area or sometimes a scrape very close to the water. There are usually two eggs. Black-throated Divers are resident in and also winter visitors to the British Isles.

Canada Goose
Family Geese, Swans and Ducks

As the name suggests, this handsome goose is a native of North America. It only occurs in this country as a result of birds escaping from private collections over the past two hundred and fifty years.

The Canada Goose is easy to recognise: a large brown goose with a distinctive black head and long neck. It has conspicuous white face patches. Canadas fly heavily with slow wing-beats. In spring they are noisy birds, for ever trumpeting their loud 'ker-honk'.

Their food consists mainly of grass and water-weed.

They are seen in flocks mainly inland on ponds, lakes and meres, even in city parks. In winter they often move to estuaries near the coast.

The nest is a hollow lined with grasses, on the ground near water and sheltered by vegetation. There are five or six eggs.

Canada Geese are present all the year in Britain.

Common Sandpiper
Family Sandpipers, Godwits, Curlews and Snipe

Waders (shorebirds) are among the hardest to identify, but the Common Sandpiper is easier than most. It is a summer resident in the British Isles and during the breeding season it is quite a common bird of hill streams, rivers and lakes in the north and west. Your attention may first be attracted by its shrill call 'see see see'. Then the bobbing movement of the hind part of its body is noticed. Lastly, you see it is coloured brownish-grey above with white underparts and a distinct white wing-bar. It flies low over the water with flickering wings.

Common Sandpipers eat mostly animal food – insects, tiny water creatures – and some water plants.

They nest near the banks of streams, rivers and lochs. The nest is a slight hollow in the ground, lined with grasses and dead water plants in the shelter of grass or weeds. There are four to five eggs.

Common Sandpipers arrive here about the end of March and leave again in August and September. A few may remain in southern England. They winter in Africa and Madagascar.

Common Scoter
Family Geese, Swans and Ducks

This is easy to recognise because the male is our only black duck. The females are dark brown with whitish cheeks and throats. The only colour on the drake apart from black is the bright orange on the ridge of the black bill.

They are sea-ducks which come ashore to nest by lakes. The males' call is a low, musical piping.

They eat mussels, shrimps, sand-hoppers, insects, worms and the roots and buds of water plants. They are seen around the coasts mainly in winter. Small numbers of Common Scoters nest on moors near lochs in Scotland and Ireland. The nest is close to the water, a hollow in the peaty soil lined with grass, down, moss and lichen. There are usually five to seven eggs.

These ducks are resident in the British Isles, but some visit us on the way elsewhere and most are seen offshore as winter visitors.

Male Common Scoter

Female Common Scoter

84

Coot

Coot
Family Rails, Crakes and Coots

Coots are distinctive as they are black all over except for a white, shield-shaped patch above the white bill. Like Grebes, Coots have lobed toes (*see* Black-necked Grebe). They are diving birds, tipping up and disappearing under the water to collect food, sometimes for as much as half a minute. They are aggressive, quarrelsome birds and fight with feet and wings. The heavy flight is usually low over the water with legs trailing.

The call is a loud, high-pitched 'kowk'. Coots eat chiefly vegetable matter, mainly water plants. They also eat tiny water creatures, earthworms, eggs and the chicks of other birds.

The large nest of reeds is built in cover near open water. There are six to nine eggs.

Coots are present all the year in the British Isles, although there is some north to south movement in winter. Gravel pits, especially in southern England, are suitable for Coot to nest in and have helped to increase the population.

Cormorant
Family Cormorants

The Cormorant is a large seabird, notable for its habit of standing on a rock or post with its wings spread out to dry.

Sometimes they are confused with Shags, but they are larger and have white chins and cheeks and in the breeding season a white patch on the thighs. Otherwise they are blackish, reptilian-looking birds with long necks and slightly hooked bills. The webbed feet enable them to swim strongly under water and dive deeply for food – up to nine metres.

Cormorants are usually silent, but at the nest they make deep guttural noises. They eat fish; only a very small proportion of their diet is vegetable.

They nest in colonies on small rocky islands, on the ledges of cliffs and occasionally on trees. The nest is a mound of dried seaweed and sticks. There are usually three or four eggs.

Cormorants are present all the year in the British Isles, but some migrate as far afield as the south coast of Portugal. During the winter they may be found inland, on reservoirs.

Garganey (*Female* left, *Male* right)

Gadwall
Family Geese, Swans and Ducks

To identify Gadwall on the water, look for a small grey duck with a black rear end. When they are flying, the broad white patch or speculum on the edge of the wing (the trailing or rear end) is very noticeable. Otherwise, the Gadwall has white underparts and a fine brown and white speckling on the head and neck, a dark grey bill and yellow legs. The female Gadwall is brown like a female Mallard.

Male Gadwall

Female Gadwall

They are what is known as surface-feeding or dabbling ducks, that is, they don't dive but find their food on or near the surface of the water.

Gadwall have a lot to say for themselves, the male a 'chuckling croak' and the female a softer quacking.

They eat chiefly vegetable matter, mostly aquatic plants, but also small water creatures.

Gadwall like lakes and marsh pools, quiet streams and other places with good cover. They nest in thick vegetation near water. The duck makes a nest of down mixed with grass and other vegetation. There are eight to twelve eggs. Some Gadwall are present all the year in the British Isles, but most come as winter visitors. They are among Britain's scarcer breeding ducks.

Garganey
Family Geese, Swans and Ducks

These are very small ducks only two and a half centimetres larger than the Teal. They are surface-feeding, rare in Scotland and Wales but breeding in small numbers in England, especially in the fens of eastern England.

The males are attractively patterned with dark brown heads and necks. There is a broad white streak over the eye extending round to the back of the neck. They also have long hanging black and white feathers where the wing joins the body. A sharp line divides the breast from the speckled grey flanks. In flight, the white face stripe and bluish patches on the forewing identify the bird.

Food is young fish, frogs, worms, insects and vegetable matter. The call of the drake is a strange crackling sound, while the duck quacks like a Teal.

They nest in England in long grass where there is good cover near water. The nest is a hollow lined with grass and down. There are usually ten or eleven eggs.

Garganey arrive in March and April, leaving in September. They are our only summer migrant waterfowl.

Goldeneye
Family Geese, Swans and Ducks

These are handsome sea-ducks, the male being a conspicuous black and white bird. The head is black, glossed with green and purple, and there is a distinct round white patch between the eye and the bill. The back, tail and wings are black, but there is a white patch on the base of the wing. The female and young have chocolate brown heads, otherwise mottled grey with the white wing patch which shows as a white mark when the birds are not flying. Goldeneye have a chunky look, the big head appearing almost triangular. The eyes are bright yellow. Goldeneye are generally silent.

They are diving ducks but also feed on the surface in shallow waters. Goldeneye like sheltered bays and usually stay close to the coast.

In Britain a few pairs nest, mainly in Scotland, by lochs and rivers where there are trees. The nests are always in holes in trees, but sometimes in nest boxes; the nest is of woodchips mixed with down. The young have no difficulty in leaving the nest. They are so light and downy that they float to the ground. There are usually eight to eleven eggs.

Goldeneye are mainly winter visitors to the British Isles from Scandinavia and Russia.

Goldeneye (Female left, Male right)

Male Goosander

Goosander
Family Geese, Swans and Ducks

This is the largest of the group of fish-eating ducks called 'Sawbills'. They have long, thin hooked bills with sharp teeth. The other two we see in Britain are the Red-breasted Merganser and the Smew. Goosanders are present all the year in Scotland and parts of northern England and Wales. They are winter visitors to other parts, especially to the reservoirs of the Thames valley. They are long-bodied with red bills and red feet. The male is handsome, with his dark bottle-green glossy head, pinkish-white breast, sides and underparts and a black back. The female is smaller with a grey back and chestnut head.

Goosanders are silent birds, except when the drake is courting the duck: then he gives a soft croaking note.

They nest in holes in partly wooded places near rivers or lochs. A favourite site is in a hollow tree. There is no proper nest but the seven to thirteen eggs are laid on down. The ducklings are sometimes carried on the parent's back.

Female Goosander

Great-crested Grebe
Family Grebes

This exceptionally handsome bird came close to extermination in Britain at the turn of the century. Grebe plumes were used to decorate women's hats. Thanks to Protection laws, its numbers have now recovered. There is no mistaking the summer plumage: conspicuous black ear-tufts and chestnut frills or 'tippets' on either side of the face. They also have long and rather thin white necks and long bills. Otherwise, they have grey-brown backs, white underparts and lobed feet. The sexes are alike. The call is a loud bark.

Great-crested Grebes are famous for their complex courtship displays.

They breed on inland stretches of water and have greatly benefited from the large number of flooded gravel pits in the south. In winter most of them move to estuaries and coastal waters.

They are expert divers and eat mainly small fish and some water weed.

The nest is built of reeds and sticks piled in the water at the edge of lakes or large ponds. There are three to four eggs. After hatching, the boldly striped chicks are often carried on the back of one parent and the other brings food. Great-crested Grebes are present all the year in Britain.

Grey Phalarope
Family Phalaropes

Phalaropes are strange little birds like waders in shape, but more often seen swimming than wading and often observed far out to sea. The Grey Phalarope, in common with its relative the Red-necked Phalarope, is remarkably tame and seems to ignore people entirely. Grey Phalaropes are twenty centimetres long and in summer plumage have dark brown backs marked with buff and chestnut, chestnut underparts as well as whitish sides of the face. In winter they live up to their name when they are grey above and white below with white heads.

The female is larger and more brightly coloured than the male in this family of birds and also leaves incubation and care of the young to the male (*see* Red-necked Phalarope).

All Phalaropes have the habit of spinning round while feeding in shallow water. This disturbs small floating insects and crustacea which they pick off daintily with their needle-shaped bills.

They are rare passage migrants only – from Iceland, Greenland and Spitsbergen – to the British Isles.

Male Grey Phalarope

Grey Wagtail
Family Pipits and Wagtails

In spite of its name, this is quite a colourful bird, having a bright yellow breast, blue-grey upperparts and a black tail almost as long as its body with white outer tail-feathers. The chin and throat of the male are black in summer. It is often seen in dipping flight or perching on rocks in swift, shallow, rocky streams, also in small lakes in hilly districts, often in company with Dippers. The bird constantly flicks its tail up and down, and its call is 'tzi tzi'.

Grey Wagtails feed mainly on insects.

They breed quite close to running water, as a rule, in a hole or on a ledge. Sometimes they use the old nest of another bird, such as a Dipper. The nest is built of moss, twigs, leaves and grass lined with horsehair. There are usually five eggs.

Grey Wagtails are present all the year in the British Isles but some move south in autumn.

Heron
Family Herons and Bitterns

They are usually seen standing like grey statues in shallow water, patiently waiting for a fish to swim by. It is then promptly grabbed by the long dagger bill and swallowed. Herons are not uncommon and can be seen beside shallow rivers, lakes and estuaries.

They have grey upperparts and tail, white head and neck and a black band running from the eye to the tip of a long crest. The legs are very long and brown and the beak is yellow. In flight, Herons have their heads drawn back and the legs trail behind.

The main call, uttered both standing and in flight, is a short, harsh, 'frank'.

Their food is mainly fish, but they also take frogs, some mammals and birds, insects and worms.

They nest in colonies, usually in tall trees, and the same nest is used for several years. It is made of branches and sticks and the lining is of twigs, roots and grass. There are three to five eggs.

Grey herons are present all the year in the British Isles but visitors come to us for the winter.

89

Kingfisher

Kingfisher
Family Kingfishers

The Kingfisher's brilliant colouring, its shape and its habit of diving for fish from a branch by the side of a stream set it apart. When fishing, it sits upright with head down-turned to scan the water.

The back, head, wings and short tail are a metallic blue flashing with green; the underparts are bright chestnut; and the small feet are bright red. The long bill is shaped like a dagger. When the bird catches a fish it beats it against a stone and swallows it head first.

The Kingfisher is usually seen as a bright blue flash in low direct flight over the water. Sometimes it hovers with its body nearly vertical. It often announces its coming by a sharp, shrill call – 'chee'.

Besides small fish it also eats insects and occasionally frogs and tadpoles.

For the nest, both sexes excavate a tunnel in the banks of slowly moving streams. There are six to seven eggs.

Kingfishers are present all the year in the British Isles generally, but rare in Scotland.

Kingfisher feeding

Little Grebe
Family Grebes

This is our smallest Grebe, and often known as the Dabchick. It is usually seen on quiet, slow-moving fresh water. Its summer plumage is dark brown with chestnut cheeks and throat, but in winter the colour is paler and the throat white. The most familiar call is a whinnying trill.

Little Grebes dive constantly and eat small fish and other water creatures, insects and some weed.

They nest on small ponds, lake edges and sometimes in beds of rushes by slow-flowing rivers. Both sexes build the nest which is a mound of water-weed. There are four to six eggs. The chicks often climb on to their parents' backs.

Little Grebes are present all the year in the British Isles. In winter there may be visitors from the Continent.

90

Mallard
Family Geese, Swans and Ducks

This is our common 'wild duck'. It occurs everywhere where there is water and is the duck in the local pond. The drake has a dark green head, a white collar, a brown breast and a pale grey back, dark brown in the centre. The underparts are grey and the tail black and white with four black centre tail feathers which curl over. There is a distinctive violet wing patch edged with black and white on both the drake and the duck. She is otherwise mottled brown and buff.

She has a loud quacking call, but the drake a subdued one which sounds rather like 'quite right'.

Mallard dabble and up-end for their food, living mainly on water-weed, but also taking frogs and worms. The flight is swift and direct.

They nest in dense vegetation, mostly on the ground, but sometimes in holes in trees or ruined buildings. The duck builds the nest of grass, reeds, etc., lining it with down from her own body. There are usually ten to twelve eggs.

Mallard are present all the year in the British Isles but winter visitors build up the numbers.

Mallard (Female above, Male below)

Male Mandarin Duck

Female Mandarin Duck

Mandarin Duck
Family Geese, Swans and Ducks

Mandarins were introduced into Europe from Asia as ornamental waterfowl and now breed in a wild state in some parts of England and Scotland. They must be the world's most colourful duck. In breeding plumage, the drake has a sail-like orange fan, which stands upright on each wing and a chestnut ruff or side-whiskers. The mane is black with a broad white eye-stripe. The duck is brownish-grey with white spots on the breast and white marks behind the eye and round the bill.

Mandarins don't say much, but the drake has a sharp whistle.

They eat both vegetable and animal food.

They are woodland duck and nest in hollow trees near water, the nest being made of rotten wood and down. There are usually nine to twelve eggs.

These exotic duck are present all the year in England and Scotland but only occur in small numbers, mainly in south-east England.

Moorhen
Family Rails, Crakes and Coots

This blackish waterbird is more numerous than the Coot although it may not appear so, because it is not so often seen in winter flocks. It is slightly smaller and has a red patch or shield above the red bill. It also has a white stripe on each side and a lot of white under the tail, which it frequently flirts when swimming; it also jerks its head. Moorhens have long green legs with very long toes. Young Moorhens are brown with a greenish-brown shield and bill.

The main calls are a croak and a sharp 'kittick'.

They eat vegetable matter, but also insects, worms, slugs, snails, tadpoles and fish.

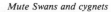
Mute Swan (Cob and Pen at nest)

Mute Swans and cygnets

Moorhens are mostly found on ponds and other small quiet stretches of water. The nest of dead reeds and water plants is usually on the ground near water. There are five to eleven eggs.

Moorhens are present all the year and also appear as winter visitors to the British Isles.

Mute Swan
Family Geese, Swans and Ducks

These stately birds now living wild in the British Isles are mostly descended from swans which were domesticated during the Middle Ages for food.

They are a familiar sight on town lakes, but as we have other wild swans in winter it is as well to say that besides its large size and its all-white plumage, the cob (the name for the male) has a large black knob at the base of the orange bill and the pen (female) a smaller knob. The neck is gracefully curved.

Although called 'mute' they are not entirely silent, but make various snorts and hisses which are heard mostly at the nest or when defending young.

They eat water-weeds and roots of water plants, also some animal food such as small frogs and toads, tadpoles, worms and molluscs.

Mute Swans build huge nests of sticks and reeds near water. There are usually five to seven eggs.

They are present all the year.

Osprey
Family Ospreys   ▲

Every summer people flock to the site at Loch Garten on Speyside, where the Royal Society for the Protection of Birds maintains an observation point from which visitors can watch the Ospreys on their nest at the top of a tall pine. At the Loch of Lowes there is another hide organised by the Scottish Wildlife Trust.

Over half a million people have visited these sites and many have seen the handsome fish-hawks plunging to the surface of a loch and rising again with a fish grasped in their talons.

Ospreys are eagle-like birds with dark chocolate brown upperparts and white underparts, a white head with a broad dark band on each side and a light brown breast band.

Their call is a short, shrill whistle, and their main food is fish.

Most nest sites in Scotland are in pine trees near lochs. The nest is a bulky pile of sticks and the same one is used each year. There are usually three eggs.

Ospreys are summer visitors to Scotland from West Africa, arriving in April and leaving in August.

Pochard
Family Geese, Swans and Ducks

This is a diving duck and seen mostly on inland waters, including reservoirs and gravel pits, especially in winter.

The drake has a bright chestnut head and neck, grey upperparts and a black breast and tail. The female is grey-brown above and paler beneath.

Pochard are rather silent birds, but the drake has a wheezy note when courting and the duck makes a harsh 'kurr' sound.

They eat mainly water-weeds, but also worms, insects, frogs and tadpoles.

Pochard nest in reedbeds on ponds and lakes, very close to the water. The nest is built up with dead water plants to above the water level and is lined with down. There are six to eleven eggs.

Some of these ducks are present all the year but most are winter visitors to the British Isles.

Male Pochard

Female Pochard

Male Red-breasted Merganser

Female Red-breasted Merganser

Red-breasted Merganser
Family Geese, Swans and Ducks

Another of the saw-billed ducks. The Merganser is smaller than the Goosander with a bottle-green head and an untidy double crest. It has a distinctive white collar above a chestnut breast and the back is grey and white. The duck is brown and grey with a white wing-bar. Note the long thin red bill which is slightly hooked and perfectly adapted for catching and gripping fish.

The birds are expert divers and underwater swimmers. They can easily stay under for up to a minute.

They are mainly silent but the ducks make a harsh 'karr' sound.

Their food is almost entirely fish, shrimps and frogs. The nest is a hollow lined with down in thick vegetation near rivers and lochs and in low-lying coastal areas.

There are seven to twelve eggs.

Red-breasted Mergansers are present all the year and many are winter visitors to coastal estuaries. They breed mainly in Scotland and Ireland with a few pairs in north-west England, and Wales.

Red-throated Diver
Family Divers

The Red-throated Diver is smaller than the Black-throated Diver. Even in winter they can be told apart because the Red-throated has a slightly up-turned bill. In summer its grey-brown upperparts are different from the striped upperparts of the Black-throated. The head is grey also and there is a distinctive red throat patch, although it can look black at a distance. In winter plumage, the Red-throated looks paler than its relative but still blackish-grey above.

The Red-throated Diver has a quacking call and a high-pitched, wild wailing.

Their legs are set far back on their bodies. This helps them when diving or swimming but they are very poor walkers. They eat mainly fish.

Red-throated Divers breed in the Highlands and Scottish islands near water. There are a few pairs also in Northern Ireland. The nest is sometimes just a flattened area in grass or it may be a heap of moss and weeds very close to the water. There are normally two eggs.

They are both residents, and winter visitors to, the British Isles. ▲

Reed Bunting
Family Buntings

Reed Buntings have recently spread from their former marshland areas into much drier country. As a result, they even turn up in some parts of the country at garden bird-tables.

They have much the same sturdy look as the Sparrow, but the male's black head and throat and white collar look very handsome. Its upperparts are dark brown and there are white outer tail-feathers. The female and young are rather drab with brown heads.

Their chief call is a shrill 'seep'.

Reed Buntings have a short, jerky flight. They eat the seeds of marsh plants and grasses, as well as insects and their larvae.

They breed, as a rule, on the ground in vegetation, in marshy areas and riversides, but recently in drier places such as chalk downs. The nest is of grass and moss, lined with fine grass and horsehair. There are four to five eggs.

Reed Buntings are present all the year in the British Isles, and they are joined by winter visitors on the east coast.

Male Reed Bunting

Female Reed Bunting

Reed Warbler
Family Warblers, Flycatchers, Thrushes, etc.

Reed Warblers are small brown birds and not often seen, as they live among the reeds. They are easily confused with the Sedge Warbler, but the Sedge Warbler has a pale buff stripe over the eye, whereas the Reed Warbler is plain brown above and light below, with a white throat.

It has a scolding alarm note 'churr' and the song is a stuttering continuous one with a tendency for each phrase to be repeated three times. It also mimics other bird song.

Reed Warblers eat marsh insects and their larvae, and spiders.

They usually breed in reeds on the edge of streams or ponds. The nest is a deep cup woven from grass around stiff reed stems. It is lined with feathers and hair. There are usually four eggs. Reed Warblers' nests are often used by Cuckoos.

They are summer visitors to the British Isles from tropical Africa, but are absent from Ireland and Scotland. They arrive in April and leave in August.

95

Ruddy Duck
Family Geese, Swans and Ducks

This bird belongs to a group of rather unusual ducks, called 'Stiff tails'. Their long stiff tail feathers act as rudders when they are swimming under water. Accomplished divers, they mainly feed on water-weed and other plants which grow below the surface.

A smallish duck, it is about thirty-eight centimetres long with a characteristic look. In the summer the plumage of the drake is quite striking. The entire body is a rich chestnut red with white under the tail. The crown is black, the face is white and the bill is bright blue. In the winter, its plumage is brown and the chestnut not so bright. The female is dark brown with a dirty white face, broken by a brown stripe below the eye.

The male has a varied and spectacular display. He beats his bill on his breast, which causes bubbles to appear on the water and also produces a hollow tapping sound. The tapping increases in momentum and the tail is cocked towards the head. He also makes a low belching noise.

The nest is a basket-like structure in dense cover in which the female lays six to fifteen white eggs.

Mostly found in the Midlands and the counties of Somerset and Avon, it is spreading to other areas.

Its true home is America; captive birds escaping from wildfowl collections in the 1960s formed the basis of the British population which is probably now in the region of three to four hundred pairs.

Male Ruddy Duck

Ruddy Duck (Female left, Male right)

Sand Martin
Family Swallows and Martins

This is a smaller bird than the Swallow or House Martin and arrives first. It is light brown above and white below with a brown band across its breast. The tail is forked, but only slightly.

Sand Martins tend to be seen in parties or flocks and scarcely ever come to the ground, except to roost. Their common sound is a sort of rippling chatter uttered on the wing.

They only eat insects caught in flight, usually over water.

Sand Martins return to their nesting sites of previous years. The nests are excavated in railway cuttings, sand pits, cliffs, the banks of rivers or similar places. The tunnel is often sixty to ninety centimetres long with the nesting chamber at the end. Both sexes drill the tunnel, using beaks and feet, and the nest itself is of straw and feathers. There are four to five eggs.

Sand Martins are summer visitors to the British Isles from the beginning of March to the end of September. They winter in East and South Africa.

Sedge Warbler
Family Warblers, Flycatchers, Thrushes, etc.

About the same size as the Reed Warbler and just as skulking and hard to see, but even a glimpse will disclose the distinct, pale buff stripe over the eye. The upperparts, too, differ as the Sedge Warbler is distinctly streaked.

It isn't always a reedbed bird, but will also nest in thickets and other dense vegetation near water.

The song is very similar to that of the Reed Warbler, but more varied, a mixture of musical notes and harsh chattering, interspersed with mimicry of other birds' songs, including House Sparrow-like chirrups. Sometimes Sedge Warblers sing at night, but could scarcely be mistaken for Nightingales.

They eat mainly insects and their larvae.

The nest is in rank vegetation or reeds near the ground. Moss and dead grasses form the foundation and the lining is of hair, willow down, grass heads and feathers. There are usually five to six eggs.

Sedge Warblers are summer visitors to the British Isles, wintering in Africa. They arrive in April and leave in August.

Shoveler
Family Geese, Swans and Ducks

This large duck is easily recognised by its huge shovel bill. It is a surface-feeder and the bill is especially adapted to collect small food particles. While swimming, the bill is often held half in and half out of the water. The drake's bottle-green head contrasts with a white breast and chestnut body. The female also has a big bill and the pale blue patch on the wing.

On land Shovelers look clumsy and those bills give them a top-heavy appearance.

They are rather silent birds but the drake has a double croaking call-note.

The food consists of animal and vegetable matter.

Shovelers breed in marshes or water meadows: sometimes in more open country, as long as it is near shallow, muddy water. There are usually eight to twelve eggs.

Some Shovelers are summer visitors to the British Isles. Our breeding birds spend the winter in France and Spain. They are then replaced here by birds which have bred in Scandinavia and Russia.

Shoveler Duck (Female left, Male right)

Slavonian Grebe ▲
Family Grebes

In breeding plumage, this grebe has a chestnut neck and flanks. The head is black and there are short ear-tufts of golden feathers which point upwards. The back is dark brown. In winter these birds have the confusing black and white plumage of the grebe family. A distinguishing feature is that the black cap of the Slavonian Grebe only reaches the top of the eye; the face, neck and breast are white, not grey as in the Black-necked Grebe.

The main call is a low, rippling trill.

Their food is varied and like the other grebes, they also eat feathers when preening and give feathers to their young. It is thought that this may help digestion. Otherwise, they eat insects, small fish and crustacea.

Slavonian Grebes are rare in Britain as breeders. They nest by inland lochs in Scotland. The nest is a mound of weeds anchored in shallow water. There are usually four eggs.

Other than our few breeding birds most of the Slavonian Grebes are winter visitors.

Smew
Family Geese, Swans and Ducks

This is the smallest of the 'saw-bills' (*see* Goosander). It is much more duck-like than its relations. The male looks mainly white, but has a black eye-patch and a black band from behind the eye to the back of the neck. Smew are usually just seen as little white ducks bobbing up and down on the waters of a reservoir in winter. Their bills are shorter and thicker than the other 'saw-bills'. They are silent birds.

In flight, the male appears more black and white; the female is smaller and her grey back and breast contrasts with the white throat and cheeks, and chestnut head.

Smew dive for small fish and also eat shrimps, snails and water beetles.

They are winter visitors and seen mainly on reservoirs, especially those around London.

Female Smew

Male Smew

Tufted Duck
Family Geese, Swans and Ducks

This is the commonest of our inland diving ducks. In winter it can be seen in large numbers on reservoirs and on ponds in public parks, where if not disturbed too much it may stay to breed.

The Tufted male is easily identified: a small black and white duck with a curious, drooping black crest. The white on the flanks is brilliant. They have beady, yellow eyes and really look rather comical. When they dive, they take an instantaneous header and bob up a few seconds later, like a rabbit out of a hat. The average dive lasts between twenty and thirty seconds. The females are brown and rather drab in comparison, and have a call like a growling 'kurr'.

Tufted Ducks feed on water plants, small fish, frogs and insects.

They breed mostly on lakes and ponds where there is plenty of cover, and like to be in flocks. The nest is close to the water, made of grass and down, and sometimes on a small island. There are eight to eleven eggs.

Tufted Ducks are present all the year in the British Isles and joined in winter by others from Iceland and northern and north-west Europe.

Whooper Swan
Family Geese, Swans and Ducks

The Whooper is larger than the Bewick's Swan and has a longer and more pointed black and yellow bill. This extends from the crown in very nearly a straight line. Seen close up, the yellow part of the Whooper's bill ends in a point and stretches beyond the nostril, whereas with the Bewick's the yellow patch ends more bluntly and is above the nostril.

Female Tufted Duck

Male Tufted Duck

The Whooper's long neck is held straight and has a slight kink at the base, which can often be noticed when the bird is swimming. The necks of both these swans are held straight, as compared with the graceful curve of the Mute. Whoopers, as their name suggests, have loud double-note trumpeting calls, often used when flying to keep contact in the flock. The young are greyish-brown.

Like Bewick's, Whoopers eat mainly water plants and seeds, sometimes grain from stubble fields and potatoes.

They are winter visitors, mainly from Iceland, and when they first arrive in Britain, their necks are often rust-coloured from the iron compounds in the lakes there. There have been a few records of Whoopers breeding in Scotland.

Whooper Swans with cygnets

Birds of Forests Mountains and Moors

Male Black Grouse

Female Black Grouse

Black Grouse
Family Grouse

Most people in the British Isles don't live near forests, mountains or moors, so these birds seem strange and exciting. The Black Grouse have display grounds called 'leks' where males joust and the females choose their mates.

The male Black Grouse, or Blackcock, has a glossy blue-black plumage and a tail in the shape of a harp-like instrument called a lyre. It also has a white wing-bar, white under the tail, and a red wattle over each eye. The female, known confusingly as Greyhen, is smaller and mostly brown, barred with black. She has a forked tail.

The Blackcock crows at the lek, and has a dove-like crooning song.

In winter these birds like to eat the buds of birch and conifer shoots, but they also take insects; in summer, leaves, seeds, berries and fruits.

They nest in woods, on heaths and on the open moor. The nest is in a scrape made by the Greyhen. There are usually six to ten eggs.

Black Grouse are present all the year in Great Britain, though very rare in southern England and absent in Ireland.

Buzzard
Family Kites, Buzzards, Hawks, Eagles, Harriers and Vultures

This dark brown hawk, with somewhat paler underparts, is at times mistaken in Scotland for a Golden Eagle, although it is considerably smaller. It has broad, rounded wings and frequently soars in slow circles with splayed wing-tips like fingers. The tail is wide, rounded and barred. When hunting in open country the bird may hover, head to the wind. Although Buzzards are splendid flyers, they spend much of the day perched on trees, posts or prominent rocks. On taking wing, they appear clumsy with a heavy flight.

The cry is a loud, plaintive mew, rather like a Herring-Gull.

Their main food consists of rabbits and other small mammals, dead lambs or other carrion, frogs, lizards and large insects.

It is by far our most common large bird of prey. The bulky nest of sticks is usually in a tree or on a cliff ledge. There are two or three eggs.

Buzzards are present all the year, mainly in northern and western Britain.

102

Male Capercaillie

Female Capercaillie

Capercaillie
Family Grouse

This is the largest of our game-birds and in a pinewood could be mistaken for an escaped turkey. It is a monster of a grey-black bird and in spring there are mock battles between the cocks, which leap into the air with their huge tails fanned. No bird makes a more extraordinary sound – once heard never forgotten. It starts with popping noises, like a cork being drawn suddenly from a bottle, and ends with a harsh shriek, as of a knife being ground.

In winter, Capercaillies eat conifer shoots, but in summer take fruit, berries and occasionally insects.

The nest which is hollow and lined with feathers, is on the ground in forests, often at the foot of a pine tree. There are five to eight eggs.

Capercaillies are present all the year in Scotland. They became extinct in the British Isles at the end of the 18th century, but were re-introduced from Sweden in 1837. They are now fairly common in the pine forests of the Scottish Highlands and in some parts of the Lowlands too.

Dipper
Family Dippers

The Dipper looks like a large Wren but it has a chocolate brown head with a white breast and throat. The back, wings and tail are a darker brown and so are the rest of the underparts; there is a chestnut band between the white breast and the white belly. The short tail is often carried cocked.

Dippers live near fast-flowing hill streams in the north and west. They have a habit of flicking the white 'third eye-lid'; this is thought to clear the eye of water, although they sometimes appear to be winking.

Their food is water insects. They sometimes walk into the water and search for food under the surface. The bird's shape, as it walks up-stream with its head stretched out, probably causes the pressure of the water to keep it down.

The Dipper's song is a Wren-like warble, but its call is a loud 'zit, zit'. Its nest is of moss and dry grasses lined with leaves, on a ledge of rock, in holes in walls, or under bridges. There are usually five eggs.

Dippers are present all the year in the north and west of the British Isles.

Female Dotterel

Male Dotterel

Dotterel
Family Plovers

This smallish plover is now a rarity and found only in the central Highlands of Scotland above seven hundred and fifty metres. It may have suffered through being very tame and easy to approach.

The white eye-stripes are distinctive as are the chestnut underparts with a white breast band. The female is more brightly coloured than the male and chases him when courting. The call is a twittering whistle.

The three eggs are laid on the ground in a hollow lined with mosses, lichens and grasses and the male is left to sit on the eggs and then tend the young. It can also give a convincing distraction display if the nest or young are threatened.

The food is mainly insects.

Dotterels are summer visitors and a few pairs breed in Scotland and Northern England. They winter in North Africa and the Red Sea area.

Golden Eagle
Family Kites, Buzzards, Hawks, Eagles, Harriers and Vultures

A Golden Eagle soaring among the peaks of the Highlands is a majestic sight. The broad wings and spread, upward-curving flight feathers have a wing span of as much as two metres. The head of the Eagle projects further beyond the line of the wings than a Buzzard, and wings and tail are relatively longer. Also, the Golden Eagle is a dark bird with golden feathers on the head and under the wings.

The soaring flight is similar to that of the Buzzard. Its calls are a thin yelp, a Buzzard-like 'twee-o' and barking cries.

It eats animal food entirely – hares, grouse, ptarmigan, carrion, sick lambs, small deer and many other mammals and birds.

Golden Eagles nest mainly on cliff ledges, sometimes using the same nest for years. Both sexes build the nest, of branches of trees and heather stems. It is lined with dead grass. There are normally two eggs.

Golden Eagles are present all the year and mainly confined to Scotland, except for the occasional pair in the Lake District.

Golden Plover
Family Plovers

The Golden Plover is a handsome bird of open moors. In summer its plumage is spangled black and gold; the face, throat and underparts are black.

At their breeding grounds, the off-duty parent often stands on a rock or peaty hummock as though on guard. It stands erect and still as a statue against the sky. If danger threatens, the bird will put on an elaborate distraction display, trailing its wing to draw an intruder away from the nest.

The cry of the Golden Plover is a sad, haunting one that seems to hold the spirit of the lonely moors.

For most people the best chance of seeing one is in autumn or winter, when they often form flocks with Lapwings and move south to farmland or estuaries. The pointed wings are then a distinguishing feature.

Their food is mainly insects, worms and spiders but they also take weed seeds. They nest in a hollow in the ground with little lining. There are four eggs.

Golden Plovers are present all the year in the British Isles.

Goshawk
Family Kites, Buzzards, Hawks, Eagles and Harriers.

This is the largest of the hawks. It has the characteristic, short, rounded wings and a long tail to help it to manoeuvre in thick cover, for it is a bird of the forest.

Goshawks are rare in Britain, although they seem to be breeding now in a few places.

If you were lucky enough to see one, it might appear to be a huge Sparrowhawk in its movements.

The plumage is brown above, white barred with brown below. As with all the hawks, the female is larger than the male and browner in appearance. They are usually silent.

They feed on medium-sized birds and mammals. The prey is killed by the grip of one foot, then eaten usually on the ground.

The large nest of sticks is often in a pine or beech tree. There are three or four eggs.

With the exception of the small breeding colonies, Goshawks are rare visitors from the Continent, mainly to the east coast.

Greenshank
Family Sandpipers, Godwits, Curlews and Snipe

This wader spends the breeding season on the moorland and near pinewoods in north Scotland. It is larger and paler than the Redshank with a longer, slightly up-turned bill and long, green legs. The upperparts are grey with dark markings, the underparts white. The flight is rapid and the white rump conspicuous.

Greenshanks move south in autumn on migration and may then be seen on marshes and estuaries. When disturbed the call is a loud, ringing 'tew, tew, tew'.

The food is mainly animal matter – insects, shrimps, small fish and crabs, small frogs and tadpoles.

The nest is a scrape lined with leaves in the heather on the moors. There are four eggs.

Greenshanks nest in northern Scotland and only a few winter in the British Isles, mainly on the Irish coast. Most spend the winter in tropical Africa. ▼

Golden Pheasant
Family Pheasants

One of the most colourful of all the pheasants, the male bird truly lives up to its name, having a golden yellow crest of fine hair-like feathers. The rump is also golden, while the body is scarlet and the wings blue. To add to this rich mixture there is a cape of orange black-bordered feathers at the back of the head, which looks like a judge's wig; this in turn conceals a glossy green mantle.

Like all ground-nesting game-birds, the female lacks the male's brilliant colouring and looks almost a different bird, with a mixture of golden buff brown and black feathering. This acts as a protective camouflage whilst she incubates her

eggs. Once incubation begins, she may sit continuously on her six to ten creamy coloured eggs for up to twenty-four days without leaving the nest for food or water. The downy chicks are active a few hours after hatching, as is common in game-birds.

Grain, seeds, berries and insects are the main types of food eaten.

This bird's true home is China, but since the 18th century many have been brought to Britain as ornamental birds. Some have since escaped from captivity whilst others have been deliberately released into the wild. Today there are probably around a thousand pairs breeding in various parts of the country though most are to be found in the Brecklands of Norfolk and Suffolk.

Male Golden Pheasant

Female Golden Pheasant

Male Hen Harrier

Female Hen Harrier

Hen Harrier
Family Kites, Buzzards, Hawks, Eagles and Harriers.

Harriers are medium-sized hawks with long narrow wings and long tails. They quarter the ground when hunting, flying only a metre or two up in seemingly lazy flight. Four or five wing-beats are followed by a short glide with wings half-raised in a shallow V.

The Hen Harrier can also take birds on the wing but, in spite of its name, hens are not especially harried. The food is chiefly birds and small mammals.

The male is a strikingly handsome bird – pale grey with black wing-tips and a conspicuous white rump. The female is much larger and brown with darker streaks, a white rump and barred tail.

The call, in the breeding area, is 'ke-ke-ke-ke . . .'

It is a bird of open moorland and in winter visits coastal areas. The nest is a hollow in the ground, often in heather. There are four to five eggs.

Hen Harriers are present all the year in Scotland and Ireland, otherwise seen as winter visitors, but a few pairs are found in England and Wales.

Merlin
Family Falcons

The Merlin is a very small falcon and the male, or tiercel, is little bigger than a thrush. It is extremely agile and dashing in pursuit of its prey, which may well be as big as itself. It is a bird of open country such as bare hills, moors and sea-cliffs.

The upperparts of the male are a slaty-blue, the underparts buff with darker streaks. The female is larger with a dark brown back and banded tail.

Merlin at nest with young

Merlins fly low over the ground with rapid wing-beats and sudden changes of direction. They feed mainly on small birds often grabbed on the ground – larks, pipits or buntings. Insects and small mammals are also taken. The prey is then taken to a plucking post before being presented to the female. The call is a 'quik-ik-ik-ik'.

The nest is usually on the ground, just a scrape among thick vegetation, where four to five eggs are laid.

Merlins are present all the year in the north and west of Britain; in the south it is a winter visitor.

Male Merlin

107

Ptarmigan
Family Grouse

The Ptarmigan is a strange game-bird of the Scottish mountains and seldom seen below six hundred metres. To help it to survive on the snow-covered ground in winter, its plumage changes to white except for black on the tail. In summer it is pale brown, only the wings remain white. The male has a black mark through the eye. In all plumages there is a red wattle over the eye, larger in the male than in the female, and the legs are feathered white.

They move down from the mountain tops in the mornings to feed on the shoots and leaves of mountain plants such as crowberry, bilberry and heather. A few insects are also taken. The call is a croaking sound.

The nest is a hollow on the ground, near a rock, to give some protection from the fierce gales. There are usually from five to nine eggs.

Ptarmigan are present all the year, but only in the Scottish mountains.

Red Grouse
Family Grouse

The Red Grouse is essentially a bird of the heather moors, as it relies on ling heather for its food all the year round. The male's body is dark red-brown with a blackish tail and wing-tips; the female is browner and more barred. The male has a prominent red wattle over the eye.

Unless the bird can find a territory where heather is plentiful, it becomes diseased or an easy prey to predators through weakness.

The cocks have a dramatic courtship display leaping into the air, stretching out their necks and fanning their tails to impress other males and mark their territories. As they do so, they challenge rivals with a call that sounds very like 'go-back, go-back'.

On the high moors, drifting snow sometimes threatens to bury the grouse and they then have to keep treading with their feathered feet. Another threat comes from the Hooded Crow, which is a great egg-thief.

Male Ptarmigan

Female Ptarmigan

Male Red Grouse

The nest is a scrape in the heather. There are usually six to nine eggs.

Red Grouse are present all the year, but are absent from Southern England except the South West.

Red Kite
Family Kites, Buzzards, Hawks, Eagles, Harriers and Vultures

Up to the end of the 18th century in London these birds could be seen everywhere for they were useful street scavengers and quite common all over Britain. After that time, owing to the intensive protection of game-birds, they gradually became extinct in England and Scotland. Only a small colony remained in the wooded hills of Wales where there were no game-keepers; perhaps only a dozen pairs were left by the beginning of the 20th century. Red Kites are now carefully protected by the Kite Committee and by the RSPB.

They have deeply forked tails and a characteristic flight: they seem to float in the air on long, slender, angled wings. This tireless flight gave a name to the toy flown on a string. The call is 'weeoo-weeoo'.

The upperparts are dark brown, the underparts foxy red with dark streaks and the head is grey, also streaked.

Their food is all animal – mammals, birds, frogs and worms.

They nest in oakwoods, the nest being of sticks strengthened by earth. There are two to three eggs.

A few Red Kites are present all the year, but only in central Wales.

Ring Ouzel
Family Warblers, Flycatchers, Thrushes, etc.

The Ring Ouzel is a summer visitor from Mediterranean countries to the wild hills, moorlands and wooded valleys of Britain, but it does not breed in East Anglia or the south-east of England.

Apart from the distinctive white crescent on the breast, it looks rather like a mountain blackbird, but, unlike its relation, the Ring Ouzel is no great singer; it is also a shy bird. The song is just a repetition of piping notes, often delivered when perched on a rock or boulder. There is also a harsh alarm call.

Like other members of the thrush family, in spring and summer it eats worms, insects and snails and in autumn, when preparing to migrate, takes berries and wild fruit.

The nest is a grass cup either on or close to the ground and often near a stream. There are usually four eggs.

Ring Ouzels are summer visitors to Britain from Mediterranean countries, arriving in late March and leaving in September. ▼

109

Female Snow Bunting

Snow Bunting
Family Buntings

The most likely place to see a Snow Bunting is along the east coast in winter. Small flocks, sometimes in company with Shorelarks, move about feeding on coarse grass seeds in rough country or on the sand dunes. At first glance, they may appear to be just little brown birds, but it is a delightful surprise to see the flash of white from their wing patches, tails and underneaths when they take-off in undulating flight. They may also be seen sometimes in hilly country inland such as the Lancashire Pennines.

They have a short, musical song sometimes delivered in flight or from a perch on a rock or boulder.

Snow Buntings only breed in Britain high up in the swirling mists of the Scottish Highlands, nesting among the rocks. In all, there are now just a few pairs. The nest is made of grass, moss and lichen and lined with hair and feathers. There are four to six eggs.

Snow Buntings are mainly winter visitors on coasts, especially in eastern England.

Snow Bunting (Female left, Male right)

Twite
Family Finches

This little finch gets its name from its call, which sounds like 'chweet'. It is a bird of high open country and breeds in the moorlands of northern England, in the western Highlands and Islands of Scotland and in Ireland. In winter they often join flocks of other seed-eating finches and buntings in bounding flight near the coast, where they feed in salt marshes and on stubble fields.

Twite (Male left, Female right)

The Twite has the look of a streaky, young Linnet, except that the cock is the only small brown bird with pink rump feathers. It has no pink on breast or forehead. Like the Linnet it has a cleft tail and its stout bill is grey in summer and yellow in winter.

The nests of grasses lined with hair and wool, are often in small colonies and built usually close to the ground in long heather. They may also be in gorse bushes or crevices in walls. There are five to six eggs.

Twites are present all the year in the British Isles.

Whimbrel
Family Sandpipers, Godwits, Curlews and Snipe

The Whimbrel looks like a small version of the Curlew with a similar, down-curved bill. Seen at close range, it has a distinguishing pale streak between the two dark bands on its head.

Apart from a few pairs elsewhere in northern Scotland, its only breeding stronghold in Britain is on the high moors of the Shetland Isles. Probably the best chance of seeing one is in spring or autumn on estuaries or almost anywhere on the coast, when small flocks on migration may turn up among the Curlews.

The Whimbrel has a quicker flight and a distinctive, rippling cry, consisting of seven clear whistling notes. The song heard on the breeding ground is not unlike the wild, bubbling sound of the Curlew.

On the coasts, Whimbrel eat small crabs, sandhoppers, shrimps and small shellfish; inland they eat insects, worms, and berries.

The nest is a scrape in the heather or rough grass on the moors. There are usually four eggs.

The Whimbrel is a summer visitor to the British Isles. Breeding is almost entirely confined to Shetland, and it winters on the African coast.

Wigeon
Family Geese, Swans and Ducks

The drake Wigeon has a most distinctive call – a penetrating whistle – 'whee-oo'. In Britain these colourful ducks breed mainly in north Scotland and only rarely south of Yorkshire. The drake has a chestnut head with a broad pale buff stripe on the crown. The upperparts are grey and the breast pinkish-brown. There is a patch of white on the forewing, which shows clearly in flight. The female is brown but also has the white wing patches.

They are surface-feeding ducks eating grasses, some grain and eel-grass on mud-flats.

Wigeon breed in moorland districts among heather or bracken near water, and occasionally on coastal marshes. Usually there are seven or eight eggs, laid in a hollow lined with down.

In winter large flocks move south and as many as forty thousand may be seen on the Ouse Washes in eastern England.

Wigeon are present all the year in the British Isles and wintering flocks arrive from Iceland and Russia.

A raft of Wigeon

Birds of Estuaries and Marshes

Avocet
Family Stilts and Avocets

With good reason was the Avocet chosen by the Royal Society for the Protection of Birds as its emblem. Not only is it exceptionally elegant, but its return to Britain as a breeding bird was a triumph for bird protection. Two hundred years ago they were quite common in eastern and south-eastern England, but then with the draining of the marshes, uncontrolled shooting, and general persecution in the 19th century, they soon ceased to breed.

After the last war, a few pairs returned to nest in East Anglia, and the RSPB promptly established reserves at their breeding sites on Havergate Island and Minsmere. These colonies are now well established and the birds also breed again on the north Norfolk coast. ▼

The Avocet is easily recognised by its distinct black and white plumage, long, thin up-turned bill and long blue legs. The flight is also distinctive with the long legs trailing well beyond the tail. Its call is a clear 'Kloo-it'.

They feed mainly on small shrimp and water insects in shallow brackish water. The long up-turned bill then sweeps from side to side in a scything movement.

On the RSPB reserves in East Anglia the salt content of the water is carefully controlled and the birds nest on especially constructed islands in the lagoons. There are usually four eggs. The nest is generally a simple unlined scrape.

Avocets are present all the year, breeding on the east coast and wintering mainly on the Tamar estuary in Devon. Others winter in Spain and Portugal.

A family of Barnacle Geese

Barnacle Goose
Family Geese, Swans and Ducks

This is one of the three '*black*' geese and is medium sized, coming between the Brent and the Canada.

It is seen in the western isles of Scotland, the Solway Firth and Ireland, as a winter visitor from Arctic breeding grounds.

The Barnacle is only slightly larger than the Brent, but can be distinguished by a white face, whitish underneath and a grey back with black and white bars. Its voice sounds like the yapping of a small dog. These geese graze on coastal grassland and feed mainly by night.

Bean Goose ▲
Family Geese, Swans and Ducks

One of the grey geese, it is the brownest and has no black barring on the breast, like the White-front with which it is sometimes seen. It has a long orange and black bill and the legs are also orange. The Bean Goose is fairly silent, but has a reedy double note that reminds some people of the baa-ing of sheep.

It roosts in marshes and estuaries and then moves to farmland where it feeds on grain, potatoes and other crops, also grass and clover.

The Bean Goose has a heavier flight than the Pink-foot or White-front but like the others there is the characteristic spiral descent from a height, called 'whiffling'.

They are winter visitors mainly to southern Scotland and the east coast of England from northern Europe and Siberia.

Bar-tailed Godwit
Family Sandpipers, Godwits, Curlews and Snipe

This is the smaller of the two godwits we see in Britain and is mostly seen on coasts in spring and autumn when migrating. Its breeding grounds are in the wet bogs of the Arctic tundra.

Bar-tailed Godwits are often seen in mixed flocks with Knot and Oystercatchers, feeding and in constant movement at the sea's edge. In winter they look rather like small Curlews with mottled grey-brown upperparts and whitish below, except that their bills are curved slightly upwards. The summer plumage is quite different. Then, the male's breast, neck and face are a rich chestnut, the female is a little paler. In flight, the white rump and barred tail are the distinguishing features.

When feeding, the slender bill is driven into the mud with a side-to-side movement seeking lugworms, sandhoppers, shrimps and other small creatures. The Bar-tailed Godwit is a rather silent bird when seen on passage. The best known call in spring sounds rather like: 'kirruck-kirruck'.

The Bar-tailed Godwit does not breed in the British Isles, but is seen on coasts in spring and autumn, when on passage to and from its Arctic breeding grounds. Some non-breeding birds sometimes remain during summer on coasts.

Bearded Reedling
Family Babblers, Warblers, Flycatchers, Thrushes, etc.

Until recently this interesting little bird was known as the Bearded Tit. This was incorrect, as it does not belong to the Titmouse family. The bird is now called the Bearded Reedling, although it has the local name of Reed Pheasant because of its long tail. Its whole life is spent among reedbeds and it is dependent on the reed seeds for its food in winter. By the end of the 19th century their numbers were much reduced owing to persecution and the reclamation of marshlands. Thanks to protection, especially at the RSPB Minsmere reserve in Suffolk, they have now recovered their numbers and are spreading to other areas.

As they live among the reeds they are not easy to see. First, they may be heard: a metallic 'ching-ching' endlessly repeated. Then, a reed-stem may sway and there suddenly is a strange little bird with tawny coloured plumage, a grey head, long black moustache like a Chinese mandarin, and a long tail.

The autumn is the best time to see them when they move about among the reedbeds in family parties like tiny gymnasts. They fly low over the tops of the reeds in whirring flight. The females are tawny with no black markings except on the wings.

The nest, of dead leaves lined with reed flower tops, is low down in the reeds and there are five to seven eggs. Two or more broods are common.

Bearded Reedlings are present all the year, mainly in the east and south of England.

Bewick's Swan
Family Geese, Swans and Ducks

These little swans are named after Thomas Bewick, the 18th-century bird illustrator. They come to us for the winter from North Russia and Siberia and stay from November to March or April. They are much smaller than our familiar Mute Swan and the two species are easy to tell apart.

The Mute Swan has a gracefully curved neck, but the neck of the Bewick's is straighter and while the Mute has an orange bill with a black knob at the base of it, the bill of the Bewick's is shorter in proportion to its size and black and yellow. The yellow pattern on the Bewick's bill varies – no two Bewick's are the same. The young, or cygnets, are greyish all over.

The Bewick's voice is soft and high-pitched, but louder and more honking when in flight. In a hard winter these swans come in considerable numbers to the fens of eastern England, to the Severn Estuary and to Ireland. ▼

Bittern ▲
Family Herons and Bitterns

The boom of the Bittern must be one of the strangest sounds in the bird world. It is rather like a distant fog horn and can carry a kilometre or more over the marshes in spring. This is the bird's love call.

By 1850 these weird birds had become extinct in Britain, largely because of persecution and the draining of marshes. In 1911 they bred again in the Norfolk Broads and there are small breeding colonies on the RSPB reserves at Minsmere in Suffolk and Leighton Moss in Lancashire and in Wales. The reason for their scarcity is that they require large areas of reedbed and swamp.

Bitterns are difficult birds to see, although about the same size as their relations the Herons. They have perfect camouflage: buff plumage, streaked with black and dark brown, long green legs and feet. When sensing danger, the Bittern freezes with neck and dagger-like bill pointing straight at the sky. It is then almost indistinguishable from the reeds. At other times it can hunch up with head drawn in and look half the size. It moves with a slow, stalking gait. When the Bittern flies heavily over the reeds its neck is drawn in and the legs trail behind. The food is varied and includes small mammals, small birds and nestlings, fish, frogs and water-weed. The nest, built of reeds and sedges, is in the reeds and there are four to six eggs. The Bittern, although rare, is present all the year in England and Wales.

Black-tailed Godwit ▲
Family Sandpipers, Godwits, Curlews and Snipe

These large waders have now returned to breed in Britain thanks to the efforts of conservation groups. They require large areas of wet meadows for nesting and the Ouse Washes in eastern England have now been secured for them. Here they enjoy complete protection and have built up a small but successful breeding colony. Pairs are also appearing in other parts of Britain, especially Scotland.

The Black-tailed Godwits are splendid birds in their breeding plumage. They are taller than the Bar-tailed Godwits, with longer and straighter bills. Heads and breasts are pinkish-chestnut and in flight they can be distinguished by broad white bars on the wings and by a broad black band on the end of the white tails. In winter plumage they are brown-grey above, light below, but can still be identified by the distinct wing and tail patterns.

The flight-call is a loud 'wicka-wicka-wicka'.

Their food consists of insects, shellfish, snails slugs and earthworms. The nest, built of dead grasses, is in a scrape among thick grass and there are four eggs.

Black-tailed Godwits are present all the year in the British Isles, mainly as migrants or winter visitors on east and south coasts of England. Some stay to breed.

Cetti's Warbler
Family Warblers

A skulking bird, it is rather dumpy looking as warblers go, often cocking its tail which gives it an almost wren-like appearance. On the other hand the dark brown rufous upperparts and the greyish white underparts could cause confusion with the Nightingale. However, it is the unusually loud explosive song which normally betrays its presence. This can be described as a 'chewee' or 'cheweeo' repeated several times. Preferring low tangled vegetation, usually near water, it also favours reedbeds and swamps where there is a plentiful supply of insects on which to feed.

The nest, built entirely by the hen bird, is well hidden and in it she lays three or four deep brick-red coloured eggs.

Perhaps better known to continental bird-watchers, this bird has only begun to nest in Britain during the last ten years or so. Most of the present breeding population is found in the south, though it is moving into other parts of the country. The unusual name of this bird honours the memory of an Italian priest and naturalist, Francois Cetti who lived in the Mediterranean region in the 18th century. ▼

Common Gull
Family Gulls and Terns

People often glance at a gull and say: 'Herring Gull' when all the time it is a Common Gull. Both have pale grey upperparts and white-spotted black wing-tips, so it is necessary to look at the main identification features in gulls – the beaks and legs. If it has a greenish-yellow beak with no red spot, and legs of the same colour, it is a Common Gull. It is also, at forty centimetres, smaller than its relative. The name is confusing because it is not our commonest gull, except in Scotland, Ireland and the north of England. The call is very similar to that of the Herring Gull, but shriller.

Common Gulls eat a variety of food, chiefly insects, earthworms and seeds on their breeding grounds; dead fish and sea creatures on the coast.

They breed in small colonies mainly on hills and moorland, although the only colony in southern England is in Kent by the sea. The nest is on the ground, built of heather, grass or seaweed, depending on locality. There are usually three eggs.

The Common Gull is present all the year in the British Isles, but some also visit us in winter from northern Europe.

Curlew
Family Sandpipers, Godwits, Curlews and Snipe

The plaintive cry 'coor-li' from which the bird gets its name, is a wonderful sound to hear, especially at night. This is the largest of our waders with an unmistakable long, down-curved bill. The Curlew looks stately as it stalks slowly among flocks of small active waders feeding on the muddy shores of estuaries. The twenty-five centimetres long bill is a splendid instrument for probing, whether in mud, on grazing land or bogs. The bird has a varied diet of small shellfish, shrimps and worms, insects, berries, weed seeds and occasionally grain.

The flight is fast and direct with slow wing-beats, rather like a gull. In spring at the breeding ground, the Curlew gives a wonderful bubbling and trilling song which may be heard over the open moor, rough pastures, marshes, meadows or sand dunes. The nest is a large, deep, hollow in the ground lined with grasses. There are normally four eggs.

Curlews are present all the year and breed almost everywhere in the British Isles except south-east England. They move to the coasts in winter. Some migrate to southern Africa.

Dunlin
Family Sandpipers, Godwits, Curlews and Snipe

When you see an estuary at low tide in winter with *waders* dotted about on the mud, you can be sure there will be many Dunlin among them, for they are our commonest waders. They are also among the smallest, and look rather 'hump-backed' little birds with long, straight, often slightly down-curved bills. In winter plumage, which is how we usually see them, they have brownish-grey upperparts and greyish breasts. In summer they are easier to identify as they have a distinctive black patch on the belly. They also have a narrow white wing-bar and white edges to the tail which show in flight. Dunlin are often

118

Greylag Goose

seen in great flocks and they swirl about on the shore like smoke blown by the wind. The call is a nasal 'dzeep'.

Their food is almost entirely animal – molluscs, insects, small crabs, shrimps, sandhoppers and worms.

Dunlin breed in the British Isles on moors in the north and west, salt-marshes and rough pastures. The nest, which is lined with leaves, is hollowed out in a clump of grass. There are usually four eggs.

Dunlin are present all the year round in the British Isles.

Greylag Goose (above)
Family Geese, Swans and Ducks

This is Britain's only breeding grey goose and the only one with an orange bill and pink legs. It is large and heavy and the ancestor of the farmyard goose, as can be told by its loud honking and aggressive hiss.

The Greylag breeds in the Hebrides and on the moors of north-west Scotland where there are scattered lochs. Landowners have also introduced it as a breeding bird to other parts of Scotland and England which it used to frequent, so its breeding range is spreading.

Most Greylags are winter visitors to Britain from Iceland. They are not always welcomed by farmers as sometimes large flocks settle on grazing land and damage can also be done to vegetable crops.

These geese are noted for forming close-pair bonds. The nest, of heather, grass and moss, mixed with down, is among heather and close to the water. There are four to seven eggs.

Greylags are mainly winter visitors, but some are present all the year in Scotland and there are breeding colonies in other parts of Britain.

Green Sandpiper
Family Sandpipers, Godwits, Curlews and Snipe

This bird is more easily identified when it flies, for then it looks like a large House Martin, showing a conspicuous white rump and black wings. As it takes to the air, it invariably calls with a musical 'klu-weeta-weet'. On the ground it looks similar to the Common Sandpiper and the Wood Sandpiper. However, compared to both these birds, it is slightly larger and always looks much darker on the back. In the summer, the dark upperparts are speckled with buffish white, but these are less noticeable when in winter plumage. The legs are greenish.

Though a shy nervous species and easily disturbed, it will quickly return to a favourite feeding area, such as a quiet backwater or shallow muddy pool where it can find plenty of worms and insects which it picks and probes for with its medium-sized straight bill.

Best known as a passage migrant, it is more frequently met with in autumn, when sometimes small groups might be found on marshes, sewage farms and by lakes and streamsides. It is seldom found along the seashore. A few stay through the winter.

It breeds in the marshy forests of northern Europe, eastwards, where as a rule, it lays its eggs in the old nest of some other species such as a Fieldfare, Mistle Thrush or Song Thrush. It has nested on a couple of occasions in Scotland. ▼

Little Ringed Plover
Family Plovers

Side by side with the Ringed Plover this less common bird is obviously smaller and slimmer looking, but when no size comparison can be made, it requires a closer view to detect such distinguishing features as the lemon-yellow ring round the eye, the flesh-coloured legs and the white line on the forehead. In flight, the best means of identification is the absence of any wing-bar and the distinct call, which is a shrill piping 'pew'.

The feeding behaviour is similar to other plovers, the bird taking a step forward to pick up some worm or other creature.

Foot-pattering on wet mud is another method whereby food is brought to the surface.

The nest is a scrape on bare ground, rarely near vegetation and is usually lined with small stones. The four eggs are greyish-buff and finely speckled with small brown spots. It often raises two broods.

A summer visitor, it was unknown as a breeding bird in Britain before 1938 when a pair nested in Hertfordshire. Favouring fresh water locations, where sandy, gravelly conditions exist, it is hardly ever seen on the seashore. Most of Britain's relatively small breeding population of around five hundred pairs is to be found in parts of south-east England and the Midlands where gravel pits, industrial spoil tips, reservoir margins and the like have been colonised over the past forty years.

Little Stint
Family Sandpipers, Godwits, Curlews and Snipe

This is the smallest of the waders and often seen in autumn on mud-flats and estuaries of the east coast among flocks of Dunlin, Curlew, Sandpipers and Ringed Plovers. They are grey above and white below with short, straight bills. In autumn Little Stints move south from their Arctic breeding grounds in Lapland to winter quarters in the Camargue or southern Africa and the east coast of Britain is then a staging point. They are also seen occasionally on the return journey in spring.

Like several birds that breed in the Arctic, the Little Stint is very tame and can be approached quite closely, as it darts about in the mud, pecking busily at the surface rather like a Sanderling. Not very much is known about its diet, although it eats insects and plant seeds on its breeding grounds. The call-note is a short 'chit-chit'.

Marsh Harrier
Family Kites, Buzzards, Hawks, Eagles, Harriers and Vultures

This is one of the rarest breeding birds in the British Isles; in fact, in some years, the small breeding population has been confined to one marsh in Suffolk.

They are spectacular birds, forty to fifty-six centimetres long (the male smaller than the female). Harriers are long-winged, long-tailed, long-legged hawks that live in open country. The Marsh Harrier is the largest and can only exist in marshland. The male is dark brown with blue-grey wing patches and a grey tail. The head, back of the neck and breast are buff, streaked with

Female Marsh Harrier

brown, and the underparts chestnut. The female is mainly dark brown with pale buffish head and shoulders.

Their call is a high-pitched 'quee-a'.

Marsh Harriers live entirely on animal matter, mainly small mammals and birds. They fly low over the marsh when hunting, then, glide with their great broad wings raised at an angle. An interesting feature is the 'food pass' when the male carries prey towards the nest and the female flies up to take it from his talons, sometimes flipping over on her back to do so.

They breed in reedbeds, the nest being a bulky structure of dead reed stems and other vegetation. There are four to five eggs.

A few pairs breed in East Anglia, otherwise they are seen as summer visitors.

Marsh Warbler
Family Warblers, Flycatchers, Thrushes, etc.

If all birds were as hard to identify as Marsh Warblers, birdwatching would probably come to an end. They are closely related to Reed Warblers and almost identical except that Reed Warblers have the lower back reddish, while the Marsh Warbler is a uniform olive colour. This difference may be seen if the bird is an adult at close range. The juveniles, even in the hand, are almost impossible to distinguish.

The song consists of mimicry of other birds' songs and is louder and more musical than that of the Reed Warbler.

They live on the insects to be found in marshes. The nests, made of dry grass lined with roots and hairs, are usually in osier-beds and their decline in numbers may result from the neglect of the beds, which become overgrown. There are usually four or five eggs.

Marsh Warblers are summer visitors, arriving in late May or early June from Africa and leaving in August. Three-quarters of our breeding birds are in the southern and western counties of England.

Montagu's Harrier
Family Kites, Buzzards, Hawks, Eagles, Harriers and Vultures

These are small harriers with long, slender wings and tails. The male resembles the Hen Harrier in colour with grey upperparts, but there are dark bars on the wings and the rump is grey, not white. The female is brown but slimmer than the female Hen Harrier and with less white on rump.

They are among Britain's rarest breeding birds and confined to the marshes and heaths of southern England.

Montagu's Harriers are summer visitors, present from April to September, whereas Hen Harriers, which breed further north, are usually only seen in the south during winter.

The flight is buoyant and graceful as they quarter the reedbeds or heathlands. Like other harriers, they glide low with angled wings. Their food consists of small mammals, birds, frogs and also some insects and earthworms.

The nest, of rushes and grasses lined with finer material, is built on the ground in rough open country or marshes. There are four or five eggs.

Montagu's Harrier is a summer visitor to southern England from Mediterranean countries and South Africa.

Male Montagu's Harrier

Female Montagu's Harrier

Pink-footed Goose
Family Geese, Swans and Ducks

This is one of the most numerous of the British geese. Most of our grey geese are coloured grey-brown, but the Pink-foot has a dark head and neck, pale blue-grey upperparts, a small pink and black bill and pink legs and feet.

Their call, heard mostly in flight, is the familiar goose honking, but in a mixed flock an individual 'pink-wink-wink' can be distinguished.

They are winter visitors to Great Britain from Greenland and Iceland. They may be seen chiefly on the east coast but also in the Severn estuary and from the Ribble to the Solway Firth, the Clyde and some of the Hebridean islands.

They eat corn on stubble fields and sometimes damage young wheat.

Their flight habits are similar to other grey geese, but quicker than Greylag. They have the same spiral descent from a height, known as 'whiffling'.

Pintail
Family Geese, Swans and Ducks

This is one of the dabbling ducks. The male is easily identified on land by its long, slender chocolate-coloured neck and head and white breast. White strips extend from the chest on either side of the head. Otherwise it is mainly grey. In flight, the long, pointed tail is clearly seen. The female is duller in appearance.

Most of the Pintail's food is gathered by up-ending or dabbling. Their long necks enable them to feed in fairly deep water. The main food consists of seeds and plants; in summer more animal food is taken including insects and frog-spawn.

The nest is a hollow in the ground lined with leaves and down. There are seven to nine eggs.

Only the female sits.

Pintail are present all the year. Few breed, but in winter many birds arrive from Iceland and the Continent. They are given special protection during the close season.

Red-necked Phalarope
Family Phalaropes

This little bird is a rare summer visitor mainly to the east coast of England, where it is seen in early June and then again in autumn, on passage to and from its Arctic breeding grounds. It spends the winter mostly at sea off West Africa.

For a seabird it has a very gentle look. It is indeed unusual, because the normal sex roles are reversed; the females are larger and more brightly coloured. It is they who take the initiative in courtship and the male is then left to incubate the eggs and care for the young.

A few pairs of Red-necked Phalaropes nest in Scotland, particularly in the Shetland Isles on the RSPB reserve. The birds seem to have no fear of people and are therefore in especial need of protection.

They are elegant birds in their summer plumage. The head and upperparts are slate grey; the throat is white with orange on sides of neck and throat. The lobed feet are partly webbed and the bill is black and needle-like.

The food consists of small crustaceans and insects. It is strange to watch the bird feeding, as it spins round like a top to bring the food to the surface. The nest is a hollow lined with grass, near the coast or loch side in boggy ground with scattered pools. There are four eggs.

The Red-necked Phalarope is a rare summer visitor to the east and south coast of England. There is also a small breeding colony in Shetland. The bird winters at sea off West Africa.

Male Red-necked Phalarope

Female Red-necked Phalarope

Pintails (Female left, Male right)

123

Redshank ▲
Family Sandpipers, Godwits, Curlews and Snipe

This is the most common of our medium-sized waders, and conspicuous because of its wary and noisy habits. Birdwatchers know it as the bird which sees them first and alerts every other bird around with its loud, musical 'teuk-teuk-teuk'. No wonder it is called 'the warden of the marshes'.

They are grey-brown birds with long orange-red legs and bills. The upperparts are marked with black and buff and the underparts are streaked and speckled. In flight, they have a broad white trailing edge on the wing and a white rump, which is the best way to spot Redshanks.

Their food is mainly animal matter: mostly insects, small shellfish and worms. They breed in meadows, marshes, rough pasture and the edges of moorland. The nest, lined with dry grasses, is built in the middle of a clump of grass and is cleverly hidden by the twining together of grass stems. There are usually four eggs.

Redshanks are present all the year in the British Isles. They are joined on the coasts in winter by visitors from Iceland.

Ringed Plover
Family Plovers

This is quite a common little wader, nineteen centimetres long. It is plump and easy to identify, with a broad black band across a white breast and orange legs, although birds which live among mud can often look as if they have black legs. They run about a lot, then pause, bobbing their heads and tipping up to feed. Their calls are very distinctive too, the commonest being a musical 'too-li'.

Ringed Plover eat shellfish, other sea creatures and insects.

They nest on sandy shores and in estuaries, also on shingle-banks and even in sewage farms and on sandy heaths. The nest is a scrape in the ground, sometimes without nest material and sometimes with bits of shell, small stones or grass stems. There are usually four eggs.

The female is expert at feigning injury. She staggers away from the nest, trailing a wing to distract an intruder.

Ringed Plover are present all the year round the coasts of the British Isles, and show an increasing tendency to nest inland. ▼

Male Ruff

Female Ruff

Ruff
Family Sandpipers, Godwits, Curlews and Snipe

This is one of our most fascinating birds. During most of the year it is just another scaly-brown wader, but when the breeding season comes around, the males grow the most elaborate head-dresses and ruffs of coloured feathers as if by magic. They may be coloured dark purple, black, chestnut, buff or white; sometimes a mixture. Adorned in this way, they display or show off before a party of females on special display grounds, called 'leks'. Sometimes the males rush at each other and come to blows.

Outside the breeding season Ruffs are not easy to identify. Medium-sized waders, they have shorter legs and bills than Redshanks, only a narrow white wing-bar to show in flight and a white oval patch on either side of a dark tail.

They are silent birds except for a low 'to-whit' when disturbed. Their food is chiefly insects, worms and the seeds of plants.

Ruffs bred regularly in Britain up to the 1920s and then ceased to do so until 1963, when, after 41 years absence, they resumed nesting in the Ouse Washes on the Cambridgeshire/Norfolk border.

Thanks to protection, Ruffs and their females called Reeves, now nest in Britain in these water meadows which are flooded in winter. The nest, which is a hollow lined with dry grasses, is on the ground in clumps of grass. There are usually four eggs. Ruffs are present all the year in Britain, but are seen mainly as migrants passing through from the far north to Mediterranean countries and South Africa in autumn and returning in spring.

Snipe
Family Sandpipers, Godwits, Curlews and Snipe

This is a medium-sized brown wader with an exceptionally long, straight bill. Its upperparts are reddish-brown and black striped with buff. When flushed, it flies off with a harsh cry and in a zig-zag pattern. Another call is 'chipper-chipper-chipper' heard in spring. But its best known sound is its 'drumming'. This is used in aerial display. The bird flies up to a considerable height, then dives down with the outer pair of tail feathers standing out from the rest. These vibrate in the rush of air and produce a strange sound rather like the bleating of a goat. The Snipe probe marshy ground and mud with their long, sensitive bills seeking worms and insects, although some vegetable matter is taken as well.

They nest in marshy meadows, rough pastures and in wet patches of moorland. The nest is a grass-lined hollow in a clump of grass, normally near water. There are usually four eggs.

A party of Snipe is known as a 'wisp'. Snipe are present all the year in the British Isles and are joined by winter visitors from Europe. ▼

Spoonbill
Family Spoonbills and Ibises

These are heron-like waterbirds, easily identified by their white plumage and long black bills widening into a spoon-like end with a yellow tip. They are also noted for their method of feeding in the shallow waters of lagoons or marshes when they sweep their bills from side to side. In this way they filter the water to gain a varied diet. Little is known about their food in Britain, except for some vegetable matter.

On their breeding grounds in Holland they feed on molluscs, small fish, tadpoles, worms, leeches and insects. Spoonbills are silent birds except for the occasional grunt. Sometimes when excited they rattle their huge bills.

They are regular visitors to East Anglia where it is thought that they may well start breeding again before long, as they used to hundreds of years ago.

Their flight is ungainly with long neck and legs stretched out straight.

Spoonbills are seen in small numbers as summer visitors to the east coast of England and also to the south-west, where some spend the winter.

Teal
Family Geese, Swans and Ducks

This is the smallest of our ducks and the fastest flyer; although widely distributed over the whole of the British Isles, it is nowhere common. The drake can be identified by a white stripe above the wing, the chestnut head, and a curved green stripe round each eye. Otherwise it has a buff breast speckled in brown, grey flanks and a bright buff patch under the tail. The female is speckled brown and buff and has a green wing patch. In flight they often dive and wheel in tight flocks like waders.

Teal are noisy birds, the male having a whistling call 'crrick' and the female a harsh quack. When disturbed they rise almost vertically. Therefore, the description 'a spring of teal' is very apt. They are surface-feeding ducks, living on vegetable matter and a few insects and worms.

Strangely, they sometimes breed among heather on dry ground, also among bracken and in marshes, often some distance from water. The nest is a hollow in the ground lined by the duck with dead leaves and down. There are eight to ten eggs.

Teal are present all the year in the British Isles. In winter they are joined by visitors from the Continent, and Iceland.

Spoonbills

Female Teal

Male Teal

Once seen they are easily recognised by the long red bill, olive-brown upperparts streaked with black and slate-grey breast and underparts. Another useful feature is the barred black and white sides. They are the size of a small Moorhen. The best chance of seeing one is when it darts with bill lowered from one piece of cover to another.

Their food is animal and vegetable – the animal including insects, spiders, shrimps and crayfish, worms and leeches. They seldom fly for more than a few seconds, and leave their long legs trailing.

Water Rails nest in reedbeds or among other aquatic vegetation. The nest is built of dead reeds and there are usually six to eleven eggs.

They are present all the year, breeding in marshy areas of Britain. There are also some winter visitors from the north.

Water Rail
Family Rails, Crakes and Coots

This is another skulking bird, almost as difficult to see as the Spotted Crake. It does at least have plenty to say and anyone who has spent a long time near marshes and reedbeds soon learns that the weird noises heard from an invisible creature come from this species. The sounds start as a kind of grunting and finish with a pig-like squeal. ▼

White-fronted Goose
Family Geese, Swans and Ducks

This is the most numerous of the grey geese, smaller and darker than the Greylag. The 'white front' refers to the white patch at the base of the bill which is pink in the Russian race and orange in the Greenland race. It is like a white forehead. Otherwise, the birds are grey-brown with a black barring on the breast.

Their call is louder and higher-pitched than the cackle of some other grey geese and it is sometimes called 'the laughing goose'. When they are on the ground, the white front and black bars on the plumage are easily seen. The legs are orange.

They eat grass, grain and sometimes potatoes.

They are winter visitors to the British Isles from early October to April, coming to us in flocks from North Russia and Greenland. They come mostly to the western side of the British Isles – Inner and Outer Hebrides, River Severn and Ireland. ▼

Birds of Coasts and Cliffs

Arctic Skua
Family Skuas

The Arctic Skua is a sinister looking seabird with piratical ways. It specialises in harrying other seabirds in dashing flight, diving on them persistently, until the gull or tern being pursued is forced to disgorge or drop the fish it is carrying.

Arctic Skuas are mainly brown, though they vary between dark and light shades. The most important distinguishing feature is that the two central tail feathers project for eight centimetres, like spikes, beyond the rest of the tail. They have slightly hooked, blackish bills.

In Britain, they breed only in Scotland and the northern isles, on barren moors near the sea and often among the birds on which they prey, such as Arctic Terns and Gulls. At the nesting site, which is a scrape lined with grass, they are very aggressive and will frequently attack an intruder. The bird also puts on an elaborate distraction display.

There are two eggs. Arctic Skuas are principally summer visitors. Most often they are seen on passage in the autumn off the coast.

Arctic Tern
Family Terns

Even experienced birdwatchers can have difficulty in distinguishing between this and the Common Tern, especially when the birds are immature or in winter plumage. However, the buoyant, more airy flight, longer tail streamers and relatively slimmer wings should help with identification. Less obvious differences such as the greyer looking underparts of adults can only

Male Arctic Skua

be determined in good viewing conditions. The wholly blood-red bill is a major distinguishing feature in the breeding season, while the extremely short legs, compared to the longer-legged Common Tern, is another useful means of separating the two species.

On its breeding grounds the Arctic Tern is possibly more aggressive than the Common Tern, pressing home its aerial attacks with greater intent on any intruder that dares to stray into the colony.

Most colonies are to be found on coastal dunes and rocky islets where one to three eggs are laid in a scrape, which is usually lined with marram grasses, shells or small stones. The eggs are indistinguishable from those of the Common Tern.

A summer visitor, it is our most numerous tern with its stronghold in north and west Scotland.

This bird undertakes long migrations and some can cover as many as 32,000 kilometres in a year, travelling from the Arctic to the Antarctic and back.

Arctic Terns with chick

Black Guillemot
Family Auks

This is the smallest of the auks and the least numerous. Most of our Black Guillemots breed in Orkney and Shetland, where they are often known by their Nordic name of Tystie.

In summer, the plumage is most distinctive – blackish-brown except for a broad white wing patch. The body is stout and the bright red legs and feet show clearly in flight. The winter plumage is mainly white, although the upperparts are mottled black and white; the broad white wing-bar is retained. They are often seen in low, whirring flight over the water and they are excellent divers.

Instead of heading for the open sea in winter, Tysties stay close to the rocky coasts where they breed. Also, unlike the other auks, there are usually two eggs. The nest is a scrape, sometimes under boulders on the shore, or higher up in rock crevices or rabbit burrows.

The Black Guillemot is present all the year, principally in the far north and north-west of the British Isles.

Black Redstart
Family Warblers, Flycatchers, Thrushes, etc.

Like its relation the common Redstart, this little bird has a fiery tail, which it constantly flirts. The name comes from the Old English 'steort' meaning a tail. Otherwise, they have little in common; it is sooty black with a white wing patch.

The Black Redstart was not known to nest in Britain until 1923. Its stronghold is central and southern Europe. Also, unlike its relation, it nests in clefts in rock faces or cliffs. Over the past fifty years or so, it has shown a liking for industrial wastelands and put the London and Dover bomb sites to good use after the last war. There, it found plenty of nest sites in the ruined buildings and also insects in the wasteland. It has been found sometimes in atomic power stations and the bird's staccato warble has even been heard inside a jumbo-jet hangar at London Airport.

The nest is usually on a ledge or in the cranny of a cliff or wall and sometimes in a derelict building or cave. There are four to six eggs.

Black Redstarts are summer visitors to central London, where over thirty pairs now breed, and to some coastal towns from Norfolk to Sussex. They also appear as winter visitors and passage migrants.

Male Black Redstart

Female Black Redstart

Brent Goose
Family Geese, Swans and Ducks

This is the smallest and darkest of our geese and it is very largely a sea goose. The Brent is a winter visitor to estuaries and mud-flats, principally along the east coast of England. The flocks like to feed on the green eel-grass, known as Zostera.

The plumage is all black or dark grey above with small white marks on the neck. In flight, the dark body and shining white rump are easy to identify; in size, this goose is little bigger than a Mallard drake. At night or at high tide the flocks roost on the sea.

There are two races of Brent wintering in England and Ireland. The dark-breasted ones visit the east coast of England from breeding grounds in Arctic Russia and Siberia; the pale-breasted ones winter mainly in Ireland and they come from Greenland. A few pale-breasted appear in England but they are probably from Spitsbergen.

Chough
Family Crows

This most attractive member of the Crow family has sadly become quite a rare bird in the British Isles and is now confined mainly to sea-cliffs in the west and in Ireland. It seems to have a gentler disposition than most of the crows. The black plumage has a bluish-green gloss, the red bill is long, thin and down-curved; the legs are also red.

In flight the Chough is a spectacular performer with broad wings and widespread primaries. It often soars in the currents at cliff edges, sometimes dives with closed wings, and on occasions even loops-the-loop. Perhaps the bird's name should be pronounced 'chow' instead of 'chuff' because that sounds very like its most common call.

Nests are usually in holes in cliffs or caves and sometimes in ruined buildings. There are three to six eggs. The food consists mainly of insects, also worms and spiders.

The Chough is present all the year, but is now rare in the British Isles.

Eiders on seashore

Common Tern ▲
Family Gulls and Terns

Terns are sometimes known as sea-swallows because of their forked tails, narrow pointed wings and graceful flight. Five species breed in Britain and they are all summer visitors. All have pale grey backs and wings, black crowns in summer and whitish underparts. If seen at close range the best way to distinguish them is by the colour of their bills and legs. The Common Tern has a coral-red bill with a black tip and red legs. It is also more likely to be seen in the southern half of Britain.

The bird flies with bill down-turned, as it scans the water, then hovers briefly, before plunging down just below the surface. Small fish, especially sand eels are taken, also small crustaceans and insects.

They nest in colonies and usually on a sandy or shingly shore, sometimes on a salt-marsh. The nest itself is a mere scrape and there are normally three eggs. Common Terns have declined in numbers because of the exposed position of their nests. These are often washed away by high tides or suffer from disturbance.

The Common Tern is a summer visitor, principally to coasts in the southern half of the British Isles.

Eider
Family Geese, Swans and Ducks

These large sea-ducks can be identified mainly by the sloping bill which continues the line of the forehead, like a Roman nose. Also, it is our only duck species in which the male has a white back and black underparts. The top of the head is also black and so is the tail. The white breast has a pink tinge and there are apple-green patches on the back of the neck. The female is brown with blackish markings.

The principal sound the drake makes is a cooing 'ah-oo', which sounds as if it had just heard an interesting piece of gossip.

Eiders nest near the seashore, but mainly on islands off the northern coasts of the British Isles and usually in colonies. The nest is built by the duck and is usually just a hollow in the ground lined with grass and seaweed, down and feathers. This is the eiderdown for which in some parts of the Arctic the bird is 'farmed'. There are four to six eggs. The duck is very tame on the nest and on some of the island sites will allow people to stroke her.

Eiders are present all the year in the north. Visitors are also seen widely around all our coasts.

Fulmar
Family Petrels

A rather gull-like bird, it has external tube-like nostrils as do all Petrels.

Over the sea it banks and glides on stiff narrow wings just above the waves, rather like a Shearwater or Albatross.

There are two forms of this bird, the commonest one having head, neck and underparts yellowish-white and upperparts pearl-grey, with dark primaries and a pale patch near the top of the wing. The other form, the so-called Blue Fulmar, is smoky-grey in appearance and is rarely seen in British waters.

The Fulmar will often follow ships and occurs in large numbers where fish are gutted at sea or at harbour landings and sewage outfalls where any food of an oily nature can be obtained.

In the breeding season it haunts coastal areas, ranging from precipitous rocky stacks, to low crumbling earth cliffs. In any of these situations it will nest, laying its one white egg on a ledge, hollow or recess, with no additional material added.

At the nest, the adult defends egg or young by spitting out an evil-smelling oily fluid.

Mainly a summer visitor, it arrives at its nesting site in the early part of the year, leaving for the open sea in August or September. This bird has increased phenomenally this century. At one time its stronghold in Britain was the remote island of St Kilda and before 1878 it nested nowhere else.

It now nests on virtually every suitable site around the coast of Britain.

Gannet
Family Gannets

This is the largest of our seabirds – shining white with long, narrow, black-tipped wings and a long, dagger-like bill which is bluish-white. In flight, they have cigar-shaped bodies and their wings span up to two metres. It is a great spectacle to watch Gannets diving for fish, sometimes from heights up to thirty-three metres. They plunge down almost vertically, wings folded back like an arrow head.

There are sixteen established breeding colonies mostly on lonely, flat-topped islands around Britain with about 140,000 pairs, that is roughly two-thirds of the world's Gannets. The nests are close together on cliff ledges or flat rocks and built of seaweed, grasses and odd bits of flotsam. There is one egg, which they incubate by covering it with their huge, webbed feet.

Gannets are present all the year, mainly in the west of the British Isles. Young birds migrate south to West Africa.

Glaucous Gull
Family Gulls and Terns

This large gull is a winter visitor to the north and east of Britain from Iceland and Arctic Russia. It is roughly the size of the Great Black-back, but all white, except for silver-grey wings and mantle. The only other gull lacking black wing-tips is the smaller Iceland Gull.

At its breeding grounds it feeds mainly on small shellfish, dead fish and shore carrion. It also preys on the young of other seabirds and takes the eggs. In winter it becomes a general scavenger.

The Glaucous Gull is a scarce winter visitor to northern and eastern coasts of the British Isles.

Great Black-backed Gull
Family Gulls and Terns

This is our largest and most powerful breeding gull; an enemy to other seabirds, their eggs and young. It is similar in size to the Glaucous Gull but nothing like it in appearance. The wings and back are blackish and the legs are pale pink. It has a deep, hoarse, barking voice.

The diet is varied, mainly animal, including fish, shellfish, rats, voles and mice. It eats all kinds of carrion and will kill lambs and many seabirds with its formidable bill.

Great Black-backed Gulls nest in small colonies on flat-topped rocks, on islands and also singly on the tops of coastal cliffs. The nest is built of heather, sticks, seaweed and grass. There are usually three eggs.

Great Black-backed Gulls are present all the year, round the British Isles, except on the east coast of England and south-east coasts of England and Scotland. They are increasing in numbers but do not breed inland.

Great Northern Diver
Family Divers

This is a winter visitor to the British Isles. In northern Scotland and Shetland it can also be seen in summer. There is one confirmed breeding record for Scotland.

In breeding plumage this Diver has upperparts chequered in black and white, a black neck and head, a striped black and white collar and a very large dagger-shaped bill. In winter it often occurs inland, for example, on London reservoirs, and then it is black above and white below with a black beak.

In flight, Divers have a humped-back appearance, the head and neck being in a lower plane than the rest of the body and the webbed feet stretch beyond the tail.

The Great Northern Diver has a shrill wailing cry and also a hoarse 'kwow'. It eats mainly fish but other sea-food as well.

They nest in lakes larger than those used by the Red-throated Diver because they need a good stretch of water for taking-off. The nest is a flattened area of grass by a lake-side. There are usually two eggs.

The Great Northern Diver is mostly a winter visitor off the coasts of Scotland and eastern England.

Great Skua
Family Gulls

Largest and most powerful of the Skuas, this bird is often called the 'Bonxie', an old Norse name. About the same size as a Herring Gull but stockier, it has uniformly dark plumage with a short tail and stout hooked black bill and black legs. The broad rounded wings are not pointed like other skuas and have conspicuous white patches. These are visible at a great distance and one can easily identify it by such means.

The normal flight is gull-like, but like the other skuas, this becomes dashing and hawk-like when it pursues other birds to rob them of their food.

The Great Skua generally preys upon the larger gulls and terns and will even chase Gannets, forcing them to disgorge any fish they have caught. It will also occasionally kill and eat other birds.

The nest is a scrape or hollow in grass or heathland with perhaps some grass for lining. The eggs, usually two in number, are variable in colour from light stone to reddish-brown with dark spots or blotches.

Many will nest together, but usually the nests are well scattered. Main centres of breeding are Shetland and the Orkneys. It also nests on the Scottish mainland. The Bonxie will attack all intruders on the breeding ground.

Outside the breeding season, it ranges far out to sea, but can be seen along the coast, mainly in autumn as birds move south.

Herring Gull

Grey Plover
Family Plovers

This bird is usually seen in its drab, grey-brown winter plumage, in small groups with other waders on the shore and estuaries. It is distinctive because of its compact build, thickish neck and short stout bill. At this time, it resembles a Golden Plover except that, in flight, there are black patches under the 'armpits' of the wings. Like all plovers, when feeding it makes a short run, then pauses to look around.

Its breeding ground is in Arctic Russia and Siberia. The plumage then is very handsome. The male has a jet-black face, throat and breast with upperparts spangled black and white.

It has a human sounding three-note whistle 'tee-oo-ee'.

The Grey Plover is a winter visitor and passage migrant to the coasts of the British Isles. A few non-breeders stay through the summer.

Grey Plover in breeding plumage

Guillemot
Family Auks

This is one of the family of seabirds called Auks which dive for food and look rather like small penguins. The Guillemot's bill is long, slender and very pointed. Although the upperparts look black, they are really chocolate brown. The birds in the north of Britain are darker. Some have a narrow white ring round the eye, extending as a thin white stripe across the side of the head. These birds are called 'bridled'.

Guillemots spend the winter at sea, arriving off their breeding cliffs in February, and from April onwards crowd on to the cliff ledges, which soon become packed with birds, standing almost shoulder to shoulder. They are the most numerous of the Auks with about half a million pairs. The egg is laid on the bare rock; it is pointed at one end so that it will not roll off the ledge. The egg is held on the webbed feet and pressed against the bird's body until hatching. A tremendous chorus wells up from their cliff colonies: the call is a harsh, growling 'arr'.

Guillemots are present all the year, breeding on cliffs mainly in the north and west of the British Isles and wintering at sea.

Herring Gull
Family Gulls and Terns

The Herring Gull is one of the commonest of our gulls and has extended its breeding range from cliffs to the roofs of buildings in coastal towns, and inland to boggy places and lakes.

It has a heavy yellow slightly hooked bill with a red spot near the end, and the legs and feet are flesh coloured. In general, it is white with silver-grey back and wings; the wing-tips are black with white spots. The size is about the same as the Lesser Black-backed Gull.

The young in their first year are brown; it takes them four years to attain the full adult plumage.

Herring Gulls have a variety of wailing and chuckling notes, the commonest being 'kee-yow'. They can eat almost anything including fish offal, carrion and refuse from ships. They also take small birds, nestlings of their own and other species and eggs. They are frequently seen over farmland and rubbish dumps and roost on reservoirs.

The nests are in colonies on ledges of sea-cliffs or on buildings. There are usually three eggs.

Herring Gulls are present all the year in the British Isles; in winter there are visitors from the Continent.

Iceland Gull
Family Gulls and Terns

This winter visitor from the Arctic closely resembles the Glaucous Gull except that it is smaller. In other words, it is another white-winged gull. At close range, the breeding adult is seen to have a red eye-ring. This species also has long, slender wings which reach beyond the tail.

They are even rarer in the British Isles than the Glaucous Gull, and seen mostly in the northern isles or on the east coast.

Kittiwake
Family Gulls and Terns

This is our most numerous gull with half a million pairs breeding in cliff colonies, or increasingly, on the ledges of buildings in coastal towns. It is a true sea gull, roaming over the ocean for most of the year, and getting a good living by following the trawlers, which provide a plentiful supply of fish offal. The Kittiwake is a gentle-looking gull about the same size as the Common Gull, but slighter and with triangular jet black wing-tips. The upperparts are darker than those of the Common Gull and the flight more graceful. The legs are black and the bill yellow.

At the cliff top colonies in the breeding season the air vibrates with the deafening repeated cries of 'Kittiwayke' from which the bird gets its name.

The nest is anchored to narrow cliff ledges with mud. It is cup shaped and built of moss, grass or seaweed which often straggles over the side.

There are usually two eggs.

Kittiwakes are present all the year in the British Isles.

Knot
Family Sandpipers, Godwits, Curlews and Snipe

These medium-sized waders are great travellers, leaving their breeding grounds after the short summer in the high Arctic to stream south in hordes. Tens of thousands come to the estuaries and mud-flats of Britain and Ireland, while others move further south, even as far as New Zealand.

The ones we see are mostly in winter plumage of grey above and paler below. They are dumpy

birds and the short black bill is distinctive. When feeding they are in close packed flocks. In flight too they move as one, wheeling in unison over the water, one moment appearing dark the next light as they tilt over to show their underparts.

They are usually in flocks with the smaller Dunlin.

When seen in spring, on their way north, Knots are transformed in their handsome breeding plumage of mottled black and russet above with the underneath a rich chestnut.

Knot in winter

The name may well come from their hoarse call 'knut, knut'. Knots are winter visitors to coasts and estuaries. Some non-breeders remain in summer.

Lesser Black-backed Gull
Family Gulls and Terns

This gull resembles the Greater Black-backed Gull but is smaller and paler, having a slate grey mantle and wings and a white head, rump, underparts and tail. Another difference is the

Knots in a flock

colour of the legs which are yellow. Sometimes in winter, perhaps on rubbish tips, we see the Scandinavian form which has a black back and wings. The young are brown with paler underneaths.

The Lesser Black-back has calls similar to those of the Herring Gull, but deeper and louder.

It also has a diet as varied as that of its larger relative. Almost any animal food is taken and it also eats carrion and the young and eggs of other birds. The bird is a scavenger and often spends the winter in areas where there are rubbish dumps.

Lesser Black-backs nest in colonies, often on moors or on islands in lakes. They also nest on grassy sea-cliffs. The nest is composed of any plant matter available and is on the ground, often in bracken or heather. There are usually three eggs.

The Lesser Black-backed Gull is a summer visitor to Britain, though many increasingly spend the winter.

Lesser Black-backed Gulls

139

Peregrine
Family Falcons ▶

This is the aristocrat of all our birds of prey but, sadly, Peregrines have become rare, especially in England. There are now indications of a slow recovery in numbers probably due to a control in the use of poisonous agricultural chemicals.

Peregrines have long pointed wings and short, tapering tails. The upperparts are slate grey on the male, and the underneath is light buff barred with black. There is also a distinctive black moustachial stripe. The female is larger – browner above and more heavily barred below.

The flight consists of rapid wing-beats followed by long glides. These splendid birds soar high over their hunting territory, then dive on to their prey in a breathtaking near vertical 'stoop', when tremendous speeds are reached. The prey is mainly birds on the wing, especially grouse or pigeons, which often have their heads struck off by the impact.

Peregrines like open country with cliffs, mountains or moorland. They breed mainly on sea-cliffs in the south, but in Wales and Scotland often use inland sites. The nest is a scrape on a rock-ledge, or sometimes the old nest of a Buzzard or Raven is used. There are three or four eggs.

Peregrines are present all the year in Britain.

Puffin
Family Auks

No one who has watched a tubby Puffin come ashore with its huge beak clamped across a moustache of small fish and stump off to its burrow can help smiling. All the Auk family look

rather like Penguins with their black and white plumage and waddling walk, although they are not related. Puffins have short wings and in flight they beat them rapidly, while their bright orange legs stick out behind like rudders.

Black above and white below is the pattern, but the feature which gives the bird its clown-like look is the fantastic triangular-shaped bill with its pattern of blue, yellow and red.

The Puffin is not a noisy bird but has a gruff voice and growls – 'arr'.

The food is mainly animal, mostly small fish and shellfish.

Puffins nest in colonies on the turfy slopes of cliffs and hillsides. They dig their own burrows with their pick-axe bills or use rabbit burrows. There is only one egg.

Puffins are present all the year, round the coasts. Most spend the winter in the North Atlantic. ▼

Raven
Family Crows

This is the largest of the crows. Although once common scavengers, Ravens are now mainly confined to the hills and sea-cliffs in the north and west of Britain.

They are glossy black with huge heads and massive bills; in flight, the wings are broad with

the primaries spread. An important distinguishing feature is the wedge-shaped tail. In spring pairs of Ravens put on impressive aerobatic displays, tumbling about in the air and every now and again flying upside down. Their call is a deep, hoarse 'prruk-prruk'.

They eat almost anything especially carrion, small animals, seed, fruit and the eggs and young of other birds. A large nest of sticks is built on a high ledge or sometimes in a tree. There are four to six eggs.

Ravens are present all the year in the north and west of Britain.

Razorbill
Family Auks

The Razorbill is about the same size as the Guillemot but stouter and black and white. It has a curious broad, flat bill with a vertical white line; another line runs from the base of the bill to the eye. The tail is pointed and there is a narrow white wing-stripe.

Like all the Auks they are expert swimmers and divers, reaching depths of six metres. They can remain underwater for nearly a minute. Their food is fish and small sea creatures.

They are often seen on the same cliffs as Guillemots and make a similar growling sound, but there are far fewer of them. Razorbills usually nest in the clefts and crevices of cliffs, although ledges are also used. There is one egg.

Razorbills are present all the year, breeding on cliffs in the north and west of the British Isles. The winters are spent at sea, where large flocks will together form 'rafts'.

Red-necked Grebe
Family Grebes

This is a smaller version of the Great-crested Grebe and a scarce winter visitor from its breeding grounds in northern Europe mainly to eastern coastal waters.

It can be distinguished by the shorter, thicker neck and the rounder outline of the head. At closer range, the bill is seen to be black and yellow at the base. The neck is grey with grey mottling on the breast. In summer at its northern nesting place the Red-necked Grebe is a handsome bird with a black crown, whitish cheeks, a chestnut neck and two tiny black ear-tufts.

With us it is usually seen off the east coast in winter or in tidal estuaries. It occasionally turns up on waters inland especially after bad weather.

Red-necked Grebes are scarce winter visitors to the British Isles.

Rock Pipit ▶
Family Pipits and Wagtails

Rock Pipits are larger and darker than Meadow Pipits and they are seldom seen far from rocky shores in the breeding season. In winter they move to mud-banks and estuaries. Another distinguishing feature is that the Rock Pipit's outer tail feathers are grey instead of white.

The song is musical and delivered as the bird takes off from a rock, continuing as it glides downwards.

No other pipit will be seen searching for flies in rotting seaweed. In addition small fish and some seeds are taken.

The nest is usually in a hole or crevice in a cliff; sometimes in a wall or a steep bank and most often near the sea. There are four or five eggs.

Rock Pipits are present all the year in the British Isles principally on northern and western shores.

Roseate Tern
Family Gulls and Terns

The Roseate Tern is one of our rarest breeding seabirds. They could be confused with Common or Arctic Terns, but have a different call-note: a long harsh 'aaak' and a soft 'chu-ick'; they are also much whiter in appearance. Other distinguishing features are that their bills are black with a red base in summer but all black in winter, and there is a pink tinge on their breasts in spring, although this soon fades. The legs are red and long tail streamers project far beyond the wing-tips when the bird is perched. In flight, they are rather more buoyant than Common Terns.

Like their relatives, Roseate Terns eat small fish which they catch by diving at sea.

They nest mainly on islands in groups, but odd birds are sometimes found in the colonies of other terns. The nest is a natural hollow in rock, or sometimes a scrape among pebbles or seaside vegetation. There are one or two eggs.

The Roseate Tern is a scarce summer visitor principally to the north-east coasts of the British Isles and especially Ireland.

Sanderling
Family Sandpipers, Godwits, Curlews and Snipe

This is one of our smaller waders and seen mainly in winter on sandy shores around the British Isles. They are often in groups with other waders, but can be distinguished by their pale colour, their plumpness and their custom of darting along the tide-line, like so many clockwork toys. As with many birds that breed in the high Arctic, Sanderlings seem to have little fear and allow a very close approach. When alarmed they will often patter away along the shore rather than take wing.

The winter plumage is a white head and underparts with pale grey upperparts and black shoulders and wing-edges. There is a conspicuous white wing-bar in flight. Sometimes Sanderlings may be seen on passage with upperparts tinted russet from their breeding plumage.

They feed on small crustaceans, including shrimps, also worms and any dead fish on the tide-line.

In flight the call is a shrill 'twick-twick'.

Sanderlings are winter visitors mainly to sandy coasts of the British Isles. They may also be seen as passage migrants.

Sanderling on seashore

Sandwich Tern
Family Gulls and Terns

This is the largest of our terns and was named after the Kent coastal town, although it has long ceased to breed there. They are heavier birds than the Common Tern with slower wing-beats and have yellow-tipped black bills, shaggy black crests and black legs. The tails are not as deeply forked as those of other terns and their general appearance is less graceful.

The call is a far-carrying 'Kirr-ick'.

Sandwich Terns

They nest in colonies around the British Isles Sandwich Terns are much affected by disturbance and they often switch their sites from year to year. They arrive in April, after wintering off West or South Africa.

The food consists of small fish and sand eels which they take by slanting dives.

The nest is a scrape and there are two or three eggs.

Sandwich Terns are summer visitors to coastal districts of the British Isles.

Sandwich Tern and chicks

Scaup
Family Geese, Swans and Ducks

This is a diving duck that at first glance looks rather like a Tufted Duck, but the Scaup is larger and the drake has a grey back. The head is black glossed with green; breast and tail are also black. It has white sides and underparts, so it is sometimes described as dark at both ends, white in the middle. The female has a broad white ring at the base of her bill but is otherwise brown.

Scaup are marine ducks and seen in the British Isles in winter, when they gather in flocks off the coasts of Scotland and the east coast of England. Their breeding grounds are in Iceland, northern Europe and Siberia, though the odd pair occasionally nests in the far north of Scotland.

On land they can only waddle clumsily, as their webbed feet are set so far back on their bodies.

Outside the breeding season they are silent birds, except for the duck's occasional harsh call – 'Karr-Karr'. The nest is on the ground near water and there are eight to eleven eggs.

Scaup are mainly winter visitors to the British Isles from the Arctic and sub-Arctic.

Male Scaup

Female Scaup

146

Shag
Family Cormorants

The Shag is a smaller and slimmer bird than its relation the Cormorant. Its black plumage with a greenish tinge has no white patches. Another distinction is the Shag's forward-pointing crest in the breeding season. It is essentially a marine bird, roosting in caves and nesting in colonies on rocky islands, cliff ledges or under boulders near the sea.

In flight it is faster than the Cormorant, more direct, and usually low over the sea.

They eat only fish. At their nests of sticks and seaweed Shags show courage by staying put and defying all intruders – croaking, hissing and pecking at them.

They are present all the year on suitable coasts and islands of the British Isles.

Shelduck
Family Geese, Swans and Ducks

The Shelduck is the largest of our ducks and exceptional in that the sexes have similar conspicuous colouring. Both have greenish-black heads, chestnut shoulders and breasts, otherwise white with black mantles and wing-tips. To complete the handsome appearance the bill on both sexes is bright red, although the female's lacks the knob at the base.

These goose-like ducks are found around all the coasts of the British Isles. They usually breed in colonies fairly close to the sea, where mud-flats are uncovered at low tide and, although they often swim, are equally at home on land.

The nest is most often in rabbit burrows and might be in sand dunes, or rough ground, perhaps on the edge of a wood or on farmland. Nests are also found under brambles or boulders and sometimes in a hollow tree. There are eight to fifteen eggs.

After hatching, the young from several broods are often cared for by female 'nurses', while the adults leave for the annual moulting migration to the Heligoland Bight area of North Germany, where they can be safe in the broad sands during the time when they cannot fly, owing to their loss of feathers.

Shelducks are present all the year around the coasts of the British Isles.

Shelduck (Two Males left, Female right)

147

Female Shorelark

Male Shorelark

Shorelark
Family Larks

The Shorelark is seen only in winter on the east and south-east coasts, often in mixed flocks with Snow Buntings. They work along the tide-line or among salt marsh vegetation and often over fields of stubble.

They are distinctive with a striking facial pattern of black and yellow and otherwise look much like Skylarks, though the brown is less streaky. Sometimes a male will be seen with the tiny black horns of his breeding plumage.

They feed on small crustaceans and molluscs, seeds and shoots.

Shorelarks are scarce winter visitors to the east and south-east coasts from breeding grounds in northern Scandinavia.

Spotted Redshank

Storm Petrel

Spotted Redshank
Family Sandpipers, Godwits, Curlews and Snipe

In the summer, this bird is easily identified by its sooty black plumage which is speckled with white, while the dark red legs appear black at a distance.

In the winter, however, it does not look so very different from the Redshank when both species have a general greyish appearance and the legs become orange coloured. Even then, the Spotted Redshank can usually be distinguished by the longer thinner bill and its feeding behaviour; wading up to its belly in water, often immersing its head completely as it searches for aquatic insects and their larvae. When it flies however, there is no likelihood of confusion between the two, for though it also has a white rump it lacks the broad white wing-bar of the commoner species and invariably utters its distinctive 'chew-it' call.

Breeding in northern Europe eastwards across Russia, small numbers of this bird pass through Britain on migration, being more frequently seen in the autumn. Most are noted along the east coast, though it does occur inland. Half a dozen would be a good number together at one time anywhere and only occasionally is it reported in double figures.

Some birds do winter along the southern and south-western coasts of England, though one or two can be found at places as far north as the Firth of Forth.

Storm Petrel
Family Storm Petrels

This is the smallest of our seabirds and a true bird of the ocean. It is blackish-brown all over, except for a white rump and pale wing-bar. The tail is short and square-ended; the bird flies low over the waves,

sometimes pattering with its webbed feet. Petrels are said to be named after St. Peter who walked on the water. They frequently follow ships and feed on plankton.

Like Shearwaters they only come ashore to breed and under cover of darkness. They nest in colonies on rocky islands, sometimes in a musty-smelling burrow, but more often under loose stones or boulders or in ruins. There is one egg.

Usually they can be heard but not seen: from under cover comes a strange purring sound with occasional hiccups. The sound has been described as 'like a fairy being sick'. Another of its calls sounds like 'terr-chick'.

Storm Petrels are summer visitors to rocky islands off the north and west coasts of the British Isles.

Turnstone
Family Plovers

Turnstones can be seen along the tide-line of rocky beaches in winter. Little is left unturned by their stout, black bills, as they search the sea-wrack methodically for the small shellfish, sandhoppers, insects and dead fish on which they feed. They are often in company with Redshanks, Dunlins and Sanderlings.

Their upperparts are mottled brown and black, with white underparts, and the legs are orange. The plumage blends with the stones and seaweed and makes an excellent camouflage. Some birds retain their brighter summer plumage when they also have a broad black breastband. It is when they fly up that they are most easily seen by the black and white pattern of the wings and the tail also shows white with a black band.

Turnstones are winter visitors from Arctic breeding grounds to rocky and stony beaches round Britain's coasts. A few non-breeding birds remain in northern Scotland.

Index   *Note: Bold figures indicate main entry and illustration*

A

Archaeopteryx	5
Arctic Skua	**130**
migration route	9
Avocet	4, **114**
bill	20
flight recognition	11
food	20

B

Beaks	6, 18-25
Bearded Reedling	**115**
Bittern	**116**
flight recognition	11
Blackbird	6, **32**
nest and eggs	26
take-off	16
Black-backed Gull, flight of	7
Blackcap	**32**
Blue Tit	**33**
Brambling	**33**
flight recognition	12
British Trust for Ornithology	8
Bullfinch	**34**
Bunting, migration of	9
Buzzard	**102**
flight recognition	11
wings	7

C

Capercaillie	**103**
Cetti's Warbler	**117**
Chaffinch	**34**
Chiffchaff	**35**
Chough	**132**
Cirl Bunting	**63**
Coal Tit	**35**
Collared Dove	**36**
Coot	**85**
beak	22
food	22
Cormorant	**85**
beak	24
flight recognition	10
food	24
nest and eggs	28
Corn Bunting	**64**
Corncrake	**64**
County Naturalists' Trust	4

D

Crossbill	36, 37
beak	18
Crow, Carrion	**62**
Hooded	**67**
Cuckoo	**37**
feet	26
migration of	9
Curlew	**118**
Stone	**75**

Dartford Warbler	**65**
Dipper	**103**
nest and eggs	27
Diver, Black-throated	**83**
beak	22
food	22
Great Northern	**135**
Red-throated	**94**
Dotterel	**104**
Duck, migration of	9
Eider	**133**
beak	22
food	22
Long-tailed	**140**
Mallard	**91**
beak	22
food	22
Mandarin	**91**
Ruddy	**96**
Shelduck	**147**
beak	22
food	22
Shoveler	6, **97**
beak	22
food	22
Tufted	**99**
landing	17
take-off	16
Dunlin	**118**
flight identification	15
Dunnock	**38**

E

Eagle, Golden	**104**
beak	25
feet	25
food	25
Eider *see* Ducks

F

Falcon, Peregrine	**142**
flight recognition	11
speed of	7
Feeding habits	6
Fieldfare	**65**
beak	18

Finches	6
Fossil remains	5
Fulmar	**134**
beak	23
flight recognition	10
food	23

G

Gadwall	**86**
landing technique	17
Gannet	**134**
beak	24
flight recognition	10
food	24
migration route	9
nest and eggs	28
Garden Warbler	**38**
Garganey	**86**
Godwit, Bar-tailed	**115**
Black-tailed	**117**
Goldcrest	**39**
beak	19
food	19
nest and eggs	26
Goldeneye	**87**
Goldfinch	**39**
flight recognition	12
Goosander	**87**
beak	21
food	21
Goose, migration of	9
Goose, Barnacle	**114**
Bean	**114**
Brent	**132**
beak	21
food	21
Canada	**83**
flight identification	15
Greylag	**119**
Pink-footed	**122**
beak	21
food	21
White-fronted	**127**
Goshawk	**105**
Grasshopper Warbler	**66**
Great Shearwater	
migration route	9
Great Tit	**40**
Grebe, family of	6
Great-crested	**88**
beak	21
feet	21
food	21
nest and eggs	28
Little	**90**
nest and eggs	28
Red-necked	**144**
Slavonian	**98**

G (continued)

Greenfinch	**41**
beak	18
flight recognition	12
Greenland Wheatear	76
migration route	9
Greenshank	**106**
Grouse, Black	**102**
Red	**108**, 109
Guillemot	**137**
Black	**131**
Gull, flight of	7
Black-headed	**82**
beak	23
food	23
Common	**118**
Glaucous	**135**
Great Black-backed	**135**
Herring	136, **137**
beak	23
food	23
Iceland	**137**
Lesser Black-backed	**139**

H

Hawfinch	6, **42**
beak	18
Hen Harrier	**107**
Heron, Grey	6, **89**
bill	20
flight recognition	11
food	20
Hobby	**67**
House Martin	**42**
flight identification	14, 15
migration of	9
House Sparrow	**43**

J

Jackdaw	**43**
Jay	**44**

K

Kestrel	**44**
flight recognition	11
nesting habits	7
Kingfisher	**90**
Kite, Red	**109**
flight recognition	12
Kittiwake	**138**
migration route	9
Knot	**138**, 139
flight identification	14

L

Lapwing	**68**
flight recognition	10
landing technique	17
nest and eggs	29
Lesser Whitethroat	**69**
Linnet	**68**
flight recognition	12

M

Magpie	**46**
Mallard *see* Ducks	
Manx Shearwater	**140**, 141
beak	24
flight recognition	10
food	24
Marsh Harrier	**121**
Marsh Warbler	**121**
Meadow Pipit, feet	26
Merganser, Red-breasted	**94**
Merlin	**107**
Migration	8
Mistle Thrush	**47**
Montagu's Harrier	**122**
Moorhen	**92**
beak	22
food	22
take-off	16

N

Navigation	8
Nightingale	**47**
Nightjar	6, **70**
beak	19
flight recognition	13
food	19
nest and eggs	29
Nuthatch	**48**
feet	26

O

Osprey	**93**
beak	25
feet	7, 25
food	25
Owl, Barn	**62**
beak	25
feet	25
flight recognition	13
food	25
Little	**69**
flight recognition	13
Long-eared	**45**
Owl, Short-eared	**73**
flight recognition	13
Tawny	**54**, 55
beak	25
feet	25
flight recognition	13
food	25
Oystercatcher	**141**
bill	20
flight recognition	11
food	20

P   PEEWIT   68

Partridge, Common	**63**
feet	26
toes	7
Red-legged	**72**
Peregrine Falcon	**142**
flight recognition	11
speed of	7
Phalarope, Grey	**88**
Red-necked	**123**
Pheasant	**70**, 71
Golden	**106**
Pied Flycatcher	**48**
Pintail	**122**, 123
Pipit, migration route	9
Meadow	**70**
feet	26
Rock	**144**
Tree	75
PLOVER GREEN	68
Plover, migration of	9
Golden	**105**
flight identification	14
Grey	**136**
Little Ringed	**120**
nest and eggs	29
Ringed	**124**
beak	24
food	24
Pochard	**93**
Ptarmigan	**108**
Puffin	**142**
beak	24
food	24

R

Raven	**143**
Razorbill	**143**
Redpoll	**49**
Redshank	**124**
flight identification	15
Spotted	**148**, 149

R (continued)

Redstart 50
   migration of 9
   take-off 16
  Black 131

Redwing 50

Reed Bunting 95

Reed Warbler 95
  nest and eggs 27

Ring Ouzel 109

Robin 5, 51
  beak 19
  food 19
  landing technique 17

Rook 72

RSPB 4

Ruff 125
  migration of 9

S

Sanderling 145

Sand Martin 96
  flight identification 14, 15

Sandpiper, Common 84
  Green 119

Scaup 146

Scoter, Common 84

Sedge Warbler 97
  migration of 8

Shag 147
  beak 24
  flight recognition 10
  food 24

Shelduck see Ducks

Shorelark 148

Shoveler, Duck 6, 97
  beak 22
  food 22

Shrike, Great Grey 66
  Red-backed 71

Siskin 51
  flight recognition 12

Skua, Arctic 130
  Great 136

Skylark 73

Smew 98
  beak 23
  food 23

Snipe 125

Snow Bunting 110

Song Thrush 6, 52
Sparrow, House 43
  Tree 55

Sparrowhawk 52, 53
  beak 25
  feet 25
  flight recognition 12
  food 25

Spoonbill 126

Spotted Flycatcher 53

Starling 6, 53

Stint, Little 120

Stock Dove 74

Stonechat 74

Stone Curlew 75

Storm Petrel 149

Swallow 54
  flight recognition 13, 15
  migration of 8, 9

Swan, migration of 9
  take-off 16
  Bewick's 116
   beak 21
   food 21
  Mute 92
   beak 21
   food 21
  Whooper 99
   beak 21
   food 21

Swift 6, 54
  beak 19
  flight recognition 13, 15
  food 19
  migration 9
  take-off 16
  wings 7

T

Teal 126, 127
  take-off 16

Tern, Arctic 130
  migration of 8
  Black 82
  Common 133
   beak 23
   food 23
  Little 4, 140
  Roseate 145
  Sandwich 146
   migration of 9

Thrush, Mistle 47
  Song 6, 52
   nest and eggs 27

Tit, Crested 36
  Great 40
  Long-tailed 46
   nest and eggs 27
  Marsh 46
  Willow 78

Treecreeper 55
  beak 19
  food 19

Turnstone 149

Turtle Dove 76

Twite 110

W

Wagtail, Grey 89
  Pied 49

Waterbirds, landing technique 17

Water Rail 127
  bill 20
  food 20

Waxwing 56
  migration of 9

Wheatear 76
  Greenland 76
   migration route 9

Whimbrel 111
  bill 20
  flight identification 14
  food 20

Whinchat 77

Whitethroat 77
  Lesser 69

Wigeon 111
  beak 23
  food 23

Willow Warbler 56

Woodcock 57
  nest and eggs 29

Woodlark 78

Woodpecker 6, 7
  nest and eggs 29
  Great Spotted 40
   feet 26
  Green 41
  Lesser Spotted 45

Woodpigeon 57

Wood Warbler 58

Wren 58

Wryneck 59

Y

Yellowhammer 79

Yellow Wagtail 79

Young Ornithologists' Club 4, 5

Acknowledgments:

Cover illustration by Wayne Ford. Illustrations on pages 4, 6 and 7 by John Leigh Pemberton; pages 5 and 9 by Gerald Witcomb, page 15 by C F Tunnicliffe, and pages 26-29 by Keith Logan.

The publishers wish to acknowledge the use of photographs as follows: pages 82 and 148, T Andrewartha/Aquila Photographics; page 67, F V Blackburn/Aquila Photographics; pages 93, 96, 140, J B Blossom/Aquila Photographics; page 104, R H Fisher/Aquila Photographics; page 112, N Rodney Foster/Aquila Photographics; pages 69 and 100, Dennis Green/Aquila Photographics; pages 138 and 139, G Huntingdon/Aquila Photographics; pages 30, 60, 80, E A Janes/Aquila Photographics; endpapers, pages 41 and 109, Horace Kinloch/Aquila Photographics; pages 37 and 140, Wayne Lankinen/Aquila Photographics; pages 64, 108, 128, 137, R T Mills/Aquila Photographics; page 119, A T Moffett/Aquila Photographics; page 106, R G Powley/Aquila Photographics; facing half title page, J Lewton Roberts/Aquila Photographics; page 93, E K Thompson/Aquila Photographics; pages 36, 37, 116, 149, D S Whitaker/Aquila Photographics; dust jacket, title page, pages 41, 86, 120, M C Wilkes/Aquila Photographics; page 102 Sid Roberts/Ardea London; pages 63, 122, 126, 140, 141, Eric and David Hosking; pages 73 and 120, Bain and Cambridge/NHPA; pages 118, 135, 137, 138, 142, J and M Bain/NHPA; page 103, R Balharry/NHPA; pages 35, 43, 46, 47, 48, 51, 55, 56, 58, 64, 68, 70, 82 , 90, 91, 95, 97, 124, 125, A Barnes/NHPA; pages 53, 62, 66, 109, 127, 132, 143, 147, J B Blossom/NHPA; pages 49, 68, 75, 79, 95, 107, 130, 136, Arthur Butler/NHPA; page 143, G J Cambridge/NHPA; pages 36, 39, 42, 49, 50, 51, 53, 59, 63, 66, 70, 71, 76, 77, 83, 84, 90, 92, 95, 106, 121, 127, 146, D N Dalton/NHPA; pages 45 and 79, Stephen Dalton/NHPA; page 56, Robert Erwin/NHPA; pages 40, 45, 55, 58, 69, 72, 73, 79, 114, 118, 127, 133, 134, J Good/NHPA; pages 67, 74, 94, 144, F Greenaway/NHPA; pages 38, 44, 57, 104, 124, 125, S J Harris/NHPA; pages 8, 33, 37, 57, 65, 68, 72, 73, 75, 77, 84, 85, 87, 88, 92, 93, 94, 96, 99, 102, 105, 107, 108, 109, 110, 114, 115, 116, 118, 122, 125, 130, 131, 133, 134, 135, 136, 139, 144, 145, 146, 148, Brian Hawkes/NHPA; page 99, C R Hedges/NHPA; pages 32, 33, 34, 38, 40, 42, 44, 48, 52, 54, 74, 89, 103, 131, 141, 147, E A Janes/NHPA; pages 39, 74, 142, J Jeffery/NHPA; page 108, R W S Knightbridge/NHPA; page 127, Stephen Krasemann/NHPA; page 135, Jerg Kroener/NHPA pages 46, 82, 103, Mike Leach/NHPA; pages 50 and 85, Lacz Lemoine/NHPA; pages 35, 43, 54, 55, 70, 98, 146, Walter Murray/NHPA; pages 104 and 111, E Murtomaki/NHPA; page 117, E Hanumantha Rao/NHPA; pages 41, 62, 88, 90, 119, Jany Sauvanet/NHPA; pages 86, 87, 91, 94, 97, 98, 99, 111, 114, 122, Philippa Scott/NHPA; page 63, Roy Shaw/NHPA; pages 53, 76, 77, 110, 132, Richard Soothill/NHPA; page 123, James Tallon/NHPA; pages 47, 53, 102, 107, 123, 148, 149, George Wall/NHPA; page 121, P Wayre/NHPA; page 78, S C Porter/RSPB; pages 36, 65, 115, 117, Michael W Richards/RSPB.

Additional text material supplied by Hilary Jarvis and Alan J Richards.

The Publishers wish to acknowledge the considerable help provided by the Royal Society for the Protection of Birds in the preparation and checking of the content of this book.

I should like to express my thanks to Dorothy Rook, former librarian, Royal Society for the Protection of Birds, for her invaluable research and assistance, which helped to make this book possible.

Robert Dougall

FOREWORD

Ian Prestt

Director, Royal Society for the Protection of Birds

Robert Dougall's great interest in wild birds developed late in life. Throughout much of his life, as broadcaster and writer, he has been concerned with putting over information in a clear and interesting way. This combination of enthusiasm for a subject with professional skills in communication makes him an outstanding choice as author of Ladybird's book of *British Birds*.

The book also benefits considerably from Ladybird's long experience of producing books for younger readers and beginners and the result is a compact, well presented, but comprehensive work of reference which will stimulate as well as inform. In addition to a description of each species, it is fully illustrated and includes summaries of special topics such as flight, migration, evolution and adaptation.

Britain can justifiably be proud of the leadership it displays in the field of wildlife conservation and education and considerable credit for this must go to the many excellent books produced in this country. This Ladybird book will undoubtedly constitute another valuable addition to existing works and will find a place in homes, schools and libraries.

First Edition

BRITISH BIRDS